FACES OF PHARAOHS

For Bernard and Mary Partridge

FACES OF PHARAOHS
Royal Mummies and Coffins from Ancient Thebes

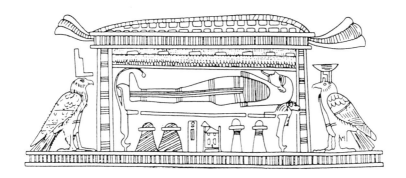

ROBERT B. PARTRIDGE

FOREWORD BY DR. A.R. DAVID

THE RUBICON PRESS

The Rubicon Press
57 Cornwall Gardens
London SW7 4BE

British Library Cataloguing-in-Publication Data.

A catalogue record for this book is available from the British Library.

0-948695-38-2 (hardback edition)
0-948695-32-3 (paperback edition)

Printed and bound in Great Britain by Biddles Limited of Guildford
and King's Lynn

CONTENTS

LIST OF ILLUSTRATIONS

Note: Unless otherwise stated, all the photographs of the mummies have been re-photographed by the author from Elliot Smith *The Royal Mummies, 1909* and all the photographs of the coffins from Daressy *Cercueils des Cachettes Royales, 1912.* Also, unless otherwise stated, all the mummies and coffins are in the collections of the Cairo Museum.

PREFACE

My fascination with things Egyptian began, I suppose, when I was nine. My family moved house; the garden of our new home had been somewhat neglected and my father spent a considerable amount of time clearing the years of growth. Whilst turning over one area, he unearthed what looked like a disc of metal. Well... at the age of nine this could only be one thing – buried treasure! The muddy, corroded lump was soon washed and scraped clean.

The find turned out to be a small copper plate, inset with brass and silver. The design on it featured a sphinx and three pyramids. The plate cleaned up surprisingly well and I remember dashing off to delve into an encyclopedia to find out something about it. Under "Egypt" I was confronted with wonderful pictures of temples, tombs and buried treasure. From that moment, I was hooked on all aspects of Ancient Egypt.

My interest in Egypt continued to grow. Three years later, my parents gave me, for Christmas, Christianne Desroches Noblecourt's book *Tutankhamen*. Several years of book collecting and reading followed, interspersed with visits to museums which had Egyptian collections. These visits were initially to museums in the United Kingdom, but later to some of the major museums of continental Europe. Eventually, in 1978, I made my first visit to Egypt, a pleasure I have now repeated many times.

After overcoming all the necessary academic hurdles, I felt able to write this book. I chose the subject of the Royal mummies and coffins mainly because I was fascinated by them, but also because there was little information easily available. The title of the book is borrowed from John Romer's *Valley of the Kings*, where *Faces of Pharaohs* is used as the heading for the chapter which describes the discovery of the tombs containing the mummies.

My idea was to reunite, on paper at least, the mummies and coffins. Most of the photographs used were originally taken in the early years of this century and many are rarely seen today.

In addition to describing the mummies and coffins, I have included chapters on mummification and on the discovery of the various tombs in which the mummies were found.

I would like to take this opportunity to thank a number of people who have helped me in my task:

- Dr. Rosalie David for running the "Certificate in Egyptology" course at the University of Manchester and providing the initial opportunity to "do" something with my long–standing interest. Dr. David was also kind enough to write the Foreword.
- Nicholas Reeves for his advice and permission to include plans and extracts from his book *The Valley of the Kings*.
- John Romer, for permission to reproduce his map of the Valley of the Kings, taken from his book of the same name.
- Donald Ryan of the Pacific Lutheran University, for his advice and for permission to include details of his work and findings in Tomb 60 in the Valley of the Kings.
- Dave Montford, who processed all my films.
- Paul Clarke and Peter Phillips for proof–reading. Peter also assisted me in a variety of other ways, which included help in taking the photographs. In addition, it was Peter with whom I discussed most of my ideas and thoughts on this work and his help and advice were invaluable.
- Anthea Page and Juanita Homan of The Rubicon Press, for their help and encouragement and for taking on an unknown author.
- the many friends who contributed towards the cost of preparing *Faces of Pharaohs* and supported and encouraged me in this work.

Finally, I have made reference to many authors and their publications in my text. I should point out that the information I have collected from these sources has been used to form my own conclusions and opinions, to which these authors may not necessarily subscribe.

Robert Partridge.

FOREWORD

The Royal Mummies are a unique and important resource for our knowledge of Ancient Egyptian culture, particularly with reference to religious beliefs, funerary customs, mummification techniques and palaeopathology. With the new display of some of these mummies in the Cairo Museum, and the realisation that much new information can be gained from them, interest in this subject has probably never been greater.

However, it is perhaps surprising, in view of the importance of these mummies and the excitement of their discovery in the two famous caches at the end of the last century (as well as other burials discovered in the Valley of the Kings) that until now there has been no single account of the Royal mummies of this period. In this book, for the first time, the author has gathered together this information, including illustrations of each mummy and their coffins. It draws together material in such a way that it will not only be a most useful reference for Egyptologists, but will also provide the general readership with a fascinating insight into the subject.

The author – Robert Partridge – undertook the Certificate Course in Egyptology which is run by the Department of Extra–Mural Studies at the University of Manchester. His final–year project for this course was a study of the Royal Mummies and Coffins of the New Kingdom, in which he was able to re–unite these mummies and their coffins and bring up to date information about current research in this field.

He was awarded a Distinction with his Certificate in 1989 and the project formed the basis of this book. He has now been able to expand his initial survey of the mummies to include all those (particularly the collection of 21st Dynasty mummies discovered in the Royal Cache at Deir el Bahri in 1881) omitted from the project.

In producing this work of reference, he has provided an invaluable addition for further studies on the Royal Mummies.

Dr. Rosalie David
Keeper of Egyptology; Manchester University Museum.

INTRODUCTION

A great deal is known to us today about most of the Ancient Civilisations of the World. This information comes to us in a variety of ways which includes contemporary written or pictorial records and archaeological investigations.

The Art of these civilisations produced representations of the human form. Most of the earliest representations have very stylised features and it is probably not until the Ancient Greek and Roman civilisations that their Art produced portraits in their truest sense.

The civilisation of Ancient Egypt produced vast amounts of sculpture and paintings for a period of over four thousand years. We know, therefore, how the Egyptians saw themselves and how they wished others to see them by their artistic representations. The features are usually stylised and only rarely does a real 'individual' emerge from the art.

We can, however, see exactly what the Ancient Egyptians looked like, for their preserved bodies have survived in large numbers, because of their funeral customs and the dry climate of the country.

Preserved bodies have been found in smaller numbers from other civilisations, although the majority of these have survived by mere chance, through natural preservation. Examples of such natural preservation are the Danish bog-bodies, preserved in peat bogs.

The Egyptians, who initially relied on a natural process, intervened to deliberately preserve their dead, often going to great lengths to ensure that the deceased had as lifelike an appearance as possible.

Thus we can look directly into the actual faces of the long-dead Ancient Egyptians. We can learn a great deal from their bodies about how they lived, what diseases and ailments they suffered during life and sometimes how they died. Much less information is available from a mere skeleton.

Modern non-destructive techniques have now been developed, with the 'Manchester Museum Mummy Project' pioneering work in this area. Many Museums which have mummies in their collections are now subjecting them to detailed study based on the non-destructive methods.

These include X-Ray, endoscopy, finger printing and the examination of microscopic tissue samples.

The new and detailed information available from the mummies, together with contemporary epigraphic and archaeological information, now means that we have a far better idea of how the Ancient Egyptians lived than for any other Ancient Civilisation.

The emphasis today is on the 'non-destructive'. Over the last two hundred years many mummies have been unwrapped and examined and at the time a great deal was learnt about the bodies. New techniques are always becoming available and much information which would have been available from these bodies has been lost because of the damage caused by previous examinations. Often material or fragments of damaged tissue were considered unimportant and were not kept. The modern approach is important, for not only is a full scientific report made of the examination, but the body, tissue samples and the wrappings are preserved and will still be available to future generations for as yet unknown tests and studies to be made.

NOTE: Over the last one hundred years there have been (and still are for that matter) many variations in the spelling of Ancient Egyptian names. The spelling and dates used in this volume are taken from the *Penguin Guide to Ancient Egypt* by William Murmane.

CHRONOLOGY

THE ARCHAIC PERIOD, Dynasties 1 and 2
(3150-2686 B. C.).

THE OLD KINGDOM, Dynasties 3 to 6
(2686-2181 B.C.).

THE FIRST INTERMEDIATE PERIOD, Dynasties 7 to 10
 (2181-2040 B. C.).

THE MIDDLE KINGDOM, Dynasties 11 and 12
(2040-1782 B. C.).

THE SECOND INTERMEDIATE PERIOD, Dynasties 13 to 17
(1782-1570 B. C.).

THE NEW KINGDOM, Dynasties 18 to 20
(1570-1070 B. C.).

THE THIRD INTERMEDIATE PERIOD, Dynasties 21 to 26
(1070-525 B. C.).

THE LATE PERIOD, Dynasties 27 to 30
(525-332 B. C.).

THE GRAECO-ROMAN PERIOD,
(332 B. C. - A. D. 323).

RULERS OF EGYPT

THE SECOND INTERMEDIATE PERIOD (END OF)

DYNASTY 17.   **(c. 1663-1570 B.C.).**

INYOTEF VII	(c. 1632)
SENAKHTENRE-TAO I	(c. 1633)
SEQUENENRE-TAO II *	(c. 1574)
WADJKHEPERRE KAMOSE	(c. 1573-1570)

THE NEW KINGDOM (c. 1570-1070 B.C.).

DYNASTY 18.   **(c. 1570-1293 B.C.).**

AHMOSE I *	(c. 1570-1546)
AMENHOTEP I *	(c. 1551-1524)
THUTMOSE I *	(c. 1524-1518)
THUTMOSE II *	(c. 1518-1504)
HATSHEPSUT	(c. 1498-1483)
THUTMOSE III *	(c. 1504-1450)
AMENHOTEP II *	(c. 1453-1419)
THUTMOSE IV *	(c. 1419-1386)
AMENHOTEP III *	(c. 1386-1349)
AMENHOTEP IV/AKHENATEN	(c. 1350-1334)
SMENKHKARE *	(c. 1336-1334)
TUTANKHAMUN *	(c. 1334-1325)
AY	(c. 1325-1321)
HOREMHEB	(c. 1321-1293)

DYNASTY 19.   **(c. 1293-1185 B.C.).**

RAMESSES I	(c. 1293-1291)
SETI I *	(c. 1291-1278)
RAMESSES I I *	(c. 1279-1212)
MERNEPTAH *	(c. 1212-1202)
AMENESSE	(c . 1202-1199)
SETI II *	(c. 1199-1193)
SIPTAH *	(c. 1193-1187)
TWOSRET	(c . 1187-1185)

At the end of the 20th Dynasty, the High Priest of Amun at Thebes claimed the powers of King in the Theban area and was portrayed with Royal insignia on monuments even though the 'real' King was still ruling from the northern City of Tanis.

For this reason, both Ramesses XI and Herihor (and then Paiankh) are shown as Rulers of Egypt. For the 21st Dynasty, two lists of Rulers are shown; those who ruled from Tanis and those who ruled at Thebes. The country was united once more at the end of the 21st Dynasty.

DYNASTY 20.   (c. 1185-1070 B.C.).

SETNAKHT	(c. 1185-1182)
RAMESSES III *	(c. 1182-1151)
RAMESSES IV *	(c. 1151-1145)
RAMESSES V *	(c. 1145-1141)
RAMESSES VI *	(c. 1141-1133)
RAMESSES VII ⎫	(c. 1133-1126)
RAMESSESS VIII ⎭	
RAMESSES IX	(c. 1126-1108)
RAMESSES X	(c. 1108-1098)
RAMESSES XI	(c. 1098-1070)

At Thebes.

HERIHOR (c . 1080-1072)
PAIANKH (c. 1072-1070)

THE THIRD INTERMEDIATE PERIOD
(c. 1069-525) (BEGINNING OF) .

DYNASTY 21   (c. 1069-945 B.C.).

At Tanis:

HEDJKHEPERRE-NESBANEBDED (SMENDES)

	(c. 1069-1043)
AMENEMNISU	(c . 1043-1039)
AHKEPERRE PSUSENNES I *	(c. 1039-991)
AMENEMOPE *	(c. 993-984)
OSORKON (the elder)	(c. 984-978)
SIAMUN	(c. 978-959)
PSUSENNES II	(c. 959-945)

At Thebes:

PINUDJEM I	(c. 1070-1055)
MASAHARTA *	(c. 1055-1046)
MENKHEPERRE	(c. 1045-992)
SMENDES	(c. 992-990)
PINUDJEM II *	(c. 990-969)
PSUSENNES II	(c. 969-945)

*Note: an * by a name indicates the survival of the mummy.*

MUMMIFICATION

Much has been written on the subject of mummification and several books which cover this in some detail are included in the bibliography at the end of this volume. Before describing the Royal mummies, it may be useful here to include a brief description of the techniques used and the possible reasons for their introduction.

One question which is not always satisfactorily answered is WHY the Ancient Egyptians preserved their dead. There must be some logical practical reasons for the introduction of this practice, which is sometimes lacking from the accepted and published theories.

During the Pre-Dynastic Period, burials were made in shallow graves in the desert sand and the heat of the ground rapidly desiccated the bodies. Most accounts of mummification in recent publications state that the Ancient Egyptians would have been aware of the preservative qualities of these shallow graves because of the exposure of bodies, possibly dug up by desert dogs or tomb robbers. This may be so, but it is likely that from an early date, the graves were protected by a small mound of stones. The stones would also have the useful practical purpose of marking the grave and would prevent other graves being made in already used ground. The relative paucity of most of the funeral goods buried with the bodies would probably not prove sufficient enticement to tomb robbers. It must be considered unlikely that many graves would have been exposed by either animal or human activities and the few which were revealed would probably have been spread over a long period of time.

It is generally assumed that embalming became necessary with the introduction of larger tombs. Bodies were now placed in deeper pits or underground chambers and were removed from the warm sand and the preservative action.

The reason for the larger tombs needs to be considered. It is often stated that the tombs were built purely to protect the bodies; this may not necessarily be the case. The tombs may have increased in size because the preservation of the body gave more time for larger monuments to be built.

With the Unification of Egypt around 3100 B.C. the society became more structured and a ruling hierarchy was established.

The rulers of the country, from the Pharaoh downwards needed tombs befitting their status. The more important the person, the larger the tomb.

The early tombs are known as 'mastabas' and are rectangular, flat-topped structures, made of either mud brick or stone, which covered the burial chamber which was made below ground.

It is assumed that these tombs evolved directly from the mounds of loose stones placed over the earlier tombs, but this evolution was amazingly rapid; in the timescale of Egyptian History, they almost appear overnight. Why? Was it the influence of new people moving into Egypt, the new stable political situation or other factors?

Foreign influence is possible, probably from Mesopotamia, although evidence for this is sparse. Certainly some of the architectural features seen in the early brick structures in Egypt are also seen in Mesopotamia, but did other countries also preserve their bodies? Evidence for this is non existent, but this does not mean that such practices were not observed, merely that no evidence has yet been found.

The Royal Tombs from Sumer were discovered earlier this century. The tombs contained many burials but the bodies were just skeletons as no other organic material survived. The excavators would not have been expecting to find any preserved bodies and may have missed small details, especially as they were no doubt greatly distracted by the vast amount of gold and jewellery which still decorated the bodies. The Sutton Hoo Ship Burial in England was also found earlier this century. To the surprise of the excavators, no body was found, although a great number of gold objects were discovered. It was only a more recent re-excavation of the site, comparison with other finds made in the same area and the use of modern scientific techniques, which established that a body had been present, but that the nature of the sandy soil had destroyed all organic matter.

This means that we cannot say for certain that the idea of mummification was not introduced to Ancient Egypt from another country.

The stability of the country no doubt played a great part in the evolution of tomb design. An organised and skilled workforce was now available to undertake the work. Whilst we know that many tombs may well have been started during the owner's lifetime, this cannot have been the case with everyone and tombs may have had to have been either started from scratch, or completed before the burial could be made.

In most countries, on the death of an individual, it is customary to wait at least a day before burial, not only to prepare for the internment, but to ensure that the deceased is actually deceased. This may sound odd, but the fear of premature burial was very real until fairly recent times. Last Wills and Testaments made in England in the 17th Century, contain instructions that burials should not be made until a specified number of days after death, to give the deceased time to 'come back to life again'. Other clauses state that the body should have some of the veins cut open, so that in the rare event of a wrong diagnosis, the supposed deceased would actually become deceased in as pleasant and painless manner as possible.

In hot climates, burial not too long after death, probably no longer than two days, is virtually essential, for a body will rapidly begin to decompose and become very unpleasant. This time can be used to prepare a simple tomb with basic grave goods and a minimum of religious ceremony. If larger tombs have to be completed before burials can take place, then some method of preserving the body and stopping this early decomposition would be highly recommended.

Some of the first attempts at mummification, involved the bandaging of the body, but why bandages? Why not just wrap the body in a sheet or enclose it in a coffin?

A decomposing body will soon begin to swell and loose its recognisable human shape. This swelling will affect all areas of the body, but particularly the abdomen, with gasses being produced by bacteria contained in the intestines. The bandaging of the body covered every extremity, with each finger and toe being individually wrapped. The tightness of the bandages would prevent or restrict, to a great extent, the swelling of the body and also exclude the air from direct contact with the body which would slow the rate of deterioration. Bandaging would also prevent the formation of blisters on the skin, caused by fluids in the body, which appear in the first stages of decomposition. Evisceration of the body (the removal of the internal organs) was practised from early times and this would have reduced the potential for the bodies to swell.

Later techniques involved covering the bandages with a layer of plaster, which further excluded the air from the body. The body would still deteriorate within the protective shell, but the outward appearance was preserved and the body would not have been too unpleasant to handle or to have around for a while until burial.

Exactly when the use of natron was introduced to completely dry the body is not known. A natural product, its preservative qualities may have been discovered by accident. This last ingredient solved all the previous problems. All moisture was now completely removed from the body; the resultant mummy was stable and could be kept unburied for a much longer period.

A number of other factors undoubtedly also come into play, all working together.

The religious beliefs and rituals were established at this time, with the story of the God Osiris, who was killed by his brother and whose dismembered body was restored to life by his wife, the Goddess Isis.

Did this myth encourage the efforts to preserve the bodies, or did the myth evolve because the practice of preserving bodies had already been established?

The religious rituals necessary for the funerals, were often lengthy, but were they long because the bodies had been preserved, or were the bodies preserved to enable the funeral rituals to be performed?

Did the belief that the body had to be preserved to ensure the deceased could enjoy the afterlife come into being because of the already proven ability to preserve the bodies, or were the bodies preserved to satisfy the belief?

In the three instances detailed above, it is likely that the practice of embalming was established first and this formed the foundation for a series of beliefs and practices, which evolved during the early Dynastic Period.

A stable body would facilitate the completion of the tomb, a period of formal mourning, preparation for the burial and the performance of the elaborate funeral rituals.

There is an almost exact historical parallel for this theory - from the Middle Ages in Europe, royal burials and burials of some nobility were always very different from those of the rest of society.

In many cultures it was often deemed necessary for the deceased Monarch to be SEEN to be deceased and for elaborate funerals to be held which were arranged and officiated over by their successor. This helped to ensure a smooth transition of power from the deceased King to the new King. Bodies would often be taken to specific sites of religious importance, before burial was made.

Embalming techniques were introduced which include evisceration and cleansing of the bodies. The viscera were packed in canopic chests, filled with bran or sawdust. The empty body cavities were also packed with bran or sawdust and the body enclosed in a winding sheet of cere cloth (a type of fine waxed cotton, which would exclude air from the body). The bodies were then placed in wooden coffins, which in turn were enclosed in lead coffins. The lead coffins were completely air-tight and bodies could then be kept for a longer period before burial. The embalming techniques of this period did not include dehydration of the body, so the bodies would still deteriorate, albeit more slowly. The air-tight lead coffins were the practical solution. The small canopic chests were also enclosed in lead. These chests were buried immediately in the vaults where the body would later be placed.

The embalming and sealing of the body in its coffin also enabled preparations for the burial to be made. Queen Mary II died in December 1694, but was not buried until March 1695, a gap of some three months. This delay was needed to complete the elaborate arrangements, which included the erection of special seating for guests in Westminster Abbey, the making of special suits of mourning for the funeral guests and even the composing of new music for the funeral service.

Interestingly enough, some of the 17th Century lead coffins for the nobility are anthropoid (body shaped) with roughly moulded faces and hands. They bear a marked similarity to Ancient Egyptian anthropoid coffins, although this similarity is completely coincidental.

In Ancient Egypt, religious, social and practical considerations probably all interacted in the formative years of the Dynastic Period and formed the basis for their expansion and development over the next three thousand years.

So, it is probable that mummification was introduced for practical reasons, initially for sanitation, rather than for preservation. Early mummies may not have been preserved for eternity, but for the period of seventy days or so needed to complete the burial. The idea of the bodies being preserved for eternity may have followed the introduction of the embalming practices, rather than being the main motive for the introduction of mummification.

THE METHODS OF EMBALMING:

The Ancient Egyptians themselves left no written accounts of the processes involved. As with most professions the skills were no doubt passed on from father to son and with no obvious need to document the process.

The information we have available to us today on the processes of mummification comes from two sources:

The first source is the writings of a Greek traveller to Egypt, Herodotus, who visited the country during the fifth century B.C. He recorded in detail his travels and his conversations with the Egyptians. Herodotus wrote at length about the burial practices and recorded three different methods of mummification. It must be remembered though that the process of mummification had been practised for at least two thousand years and that Herodotus was writing towards the end of Egypt's long history. The mummies which are described later in this volume pre-date Herodotus by hundreds of years.

The second and perhaps most important source, is the mummies themselves. Examination of a large number of mummies from all periods over the last hundred years or so, has enabled the techniques to be examined at first hand. The evidence obtained from the bodies confirms how accurate the writings of Herodotus are, although it is evident that techniques changed gradually over a period of time.

ACCORDING TO HERODOTUS:

Method One:

The brain was drawn from the head through the nostrils, using an iron hook and dissolving drugs. A special 'stone of Ethiopia' was used to incise the abdomen and the internal organs were removed. The body was cleansed with palm wine, purified with incense, stuffed with perfumes and sewn up. It was then soaked in a bath of natron for seventy days and then finally washed and bandaged.

This was the most involved and the most expensive of the methods used and would have been reserved only for the most important burials.

Method Two:

Cedar oil was injected into the body through the anus. The body was then soaked in natron. When the oil was removed, it carried away all the internal organs in a liquid state. The body was then cleansed and bandaged.

Method Three:

The body was simply washed and soaked in natron, then bandaged.

As would be expected, the Royal mummies were given the best possible treatment; broadly speaking the first method as described above. Modern experiments on rats at the University of Manchester indicate that the natron must have been applied to the bodies in a dry form. Natron will desiccate a body, but it does not work in a liquid state. The same experiments also cast some doubt on the time taken for the mummification process. Complete desiccation was achieved in a period of only forty days. The time quoted by Herodotus may have been the total time from the date of death to the date of burial. Once desiccated, the wrapping and final preparation of the body and any burial rituals may well account for the remaining thirty days.

The internal organs were sometimes replaced in the body after being preserved separately. On many occasions they were buried separately from the body in four 'Canopic Jars'. In the case of many of the earlier Royal mummies, the internal organs which were separated from the body have not survived. The canopic equipment may well have been richly made and a target for the robbers.

One major difference between Herodotus' accounts and the evidence of the mummies themselves, is that in the 21st Dynasty (1070 - 945 B.C.) the embalmers, in an attempt to restore a more lifelike appearance to the bodies, began subcutaneous packing; the introduction of mud or straw under the skin to restore some bulk to the emaciated limbs following the desiccation of the natron. The introduction of this technique was probably as a direct result of the re-burial of some of the earlier Royal mummies. During the restoration and re-wrapping of these mummies their shrivelled limbs were subjected to the close scrutiny of priests and officials who must have questioned the effectiveness of the methods used by the earlier embalmers.

The name 'mummy' is actually derived from an Arabic word of Persian origin for a body preserved in bitumen. The word for bitumen being 'mumiya'. Bitumen was not in fact normally used during the mummification processes, but the black appearance was presumed by the Arabs to have been caused by bitumen.

THE ROYAL MUMMIES

In 1881 and 1898 A.D., two important 'Caches' of mummies were discovered in Egypt. The first Cache was 'officially' discovered in 1881, but it had in fact been discovered some ten years before by the Abd er Rassul family who lived in the village of Gurna on the west bank of the river Nile at Luxor. This village is, quite literally, built on top of the ancient Necropolis and tomb-robbing was seen as a legitimate way of earning a living.

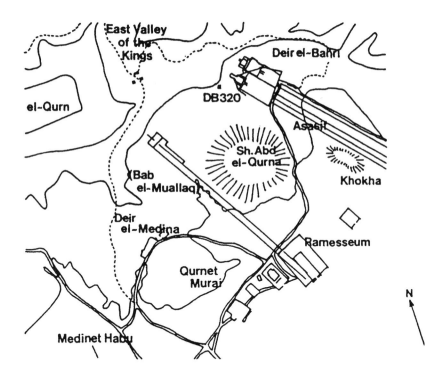

Map of Deir el Bahri showing the location of the Royal Cache. (Tomb DB 320). (Fig. 1)

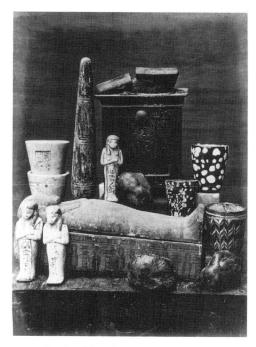

Small wooden box bearing the name of Hatshepsut (sister of Thutmose III, 18th Dynasty); five libation cups of Princess Neskhons; painted wooden emblem; small coffin of painted wood; some palm tree fruit; one ushabti of Tayuheret and two of Queen Maatkare.

Antiquities began to appear on the Black Market; these were quickly bought on behalf of the larger Museums in Europe and the United States of America who were all keen to enlarge their Egyptian Collections. Most of the items were small pieces of funerary equipment, ushabti and some papyri. It was soon evident to Egyptologists that these objects, which were of the highest quality, had come from an important unknown tomb with Royal connections. After lengthy investigations, it was eventually established that a Royal tomb had indeed been discovered, located close to the Funerary Temple of Queen Hatshepsut at Deir el Bahri and situated in the cliff face.

It was a huge tomb. Originally excavated for the burial of an Eighteenth Dynasty Queen, it was later enlarged to accommodate additional occupants. This tomb is now known as Deir el Bahri number 320 (DB 320)

Emile Brugsch was the first European and Egyptologist to enter the tomb. A shaft, about ten feet by eight, dropped forty feet into the solid rock. A small doorway gave access to a low corridor which ran northwards; this corridor was almost blocked by coffins. The corridor turned to the right and extended some seventy feet, where it opened out into a small chamber. Both the corridor and the chamber were packed with coffins, some of them quite enormous.

14

Raising his candle over the coffins, Brugsch was able to read the names of the occupants, which included Ahmose, founder of the New Kingdom, Thutmose I, II and III, Amenhotep I, Seti I and the great Ramesses II. He was stunned by the find, for here were some of the most famous and powerful of Egypt's Pharaohs. Realising that if he stumbled in the crowded tomb or passed out because of the lack of air, the candles were a real danger to the tinder-dry coffins, Brugsch left the tomb for a short while. He was later to state that he had the feeling at that moment of being an intruder a feeling shared by other archaeologists at such a time, including Howard Carter and Lord Carnarvon when they first entered the tomb of Tutankhamun.

Brugsch returned a second time and penetrated further into the tomb. He discovered that another corridor led from the chamber of the tomb. This corridor ran for nearly one hundred feet and opened out into a second chamber about twenty feet long. This chamber contained the burials of the family of the Priest-King Pinudjem of the Twenty-First Dynasty. It was objects from this part of the tomb which had first alerted Egyptologists to the possibility of a new Royal tomb.

The two visits by Brugsch lasted nearly two hours. He realised that the villagers of Gurna would know that a great treasure was about to be taken from them and he was concerned that there might be a real chance of damage to the objects and of possible violence towards the Museum Officials. The removal of the contents of the tomb would have to be completed quickly.

The clearance of the tomb was a particularly difficult exercise because of the location of the entrance in the cliff face. Under a military guard, the clearance was completed, with the help of some two hundred workmen, in just two days. The contents of the tomb, still under military guard, were taken by river to Cairo.

The speed of the tomb clearance was an archaeological disaster. No detailed record was kept of the location of individual coffins within the tomb. The order in which they were discovered could tell us much about the history of the Cache, although it is possible that the activities of the modern tomb robbers may well have greatly re-arranged the contents of the tomb.

Although the members of the Abd er Rassul family undoubtedly caused some damage and disruption, they are said to have visited the tomb on only three occasions and then only for a few hours. They were probably looking initially, for small, valuable and portable objects and would not have had the time to examine some of the large and very heavy coffins and their contents.

It is believed that the majority of the coffins were originally placed in the first chamber and that the modern tomb robbers had

Plan of Tomb DB 320; reconstructed layout (Fig 3)

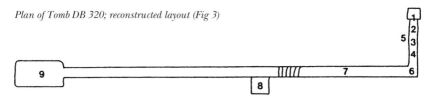

1. Coffin of Nebseni, containing a mummy.
2. A 17th Dynasty coffin, probably belonging to the Lady Rai, containing the body of Inhapi.
3. The inner and outer coffins of Duathathor-Henttawy and her mummy.
4. The coffin of Seti I, containing his mummy.
5. Various ushabti boxes. canopic jars and copper-alloy libation vessels. The ushabti boxes may have included those of Duathathor-Henttawy. The canopic jars cannot now be identified. Two sets of libation vessels were found in the tomb. One set was inscribed for Istemkheb but it is not clear which is referred to here.
6. A leather Canopy-Shrine of Istemkheb.
7. "A cluster of mummy cases...in such number as to stagger me". No reconstruction of their precise order is possible, but presumably, included in this 'cluster' were the coffin fragments of Ramesses I, the coffin of Thutmose I (usurped by Pinudjem I, but containing the mummy of Thutmose I) and the coffined mummies of Amenhotep I and Thutmose II.
8. The coffined mummies of Ahmose I, Siamun and Sequenenre-Tao. The coffin of Ahotep I containing the mummy of Pinudjem I; the coffin of Queen Ahmose-Nefertari which contained both her own mummy and the cartonnaged mummy of Ramesses III. Thutmose III and Ramesses II may well have been found in this chamber, which Maspero described as "filled up to the roof". Brugsch was quoted as having described the coffins .."standing against the walls or...lying on the floor".
9. A collection of coffins and mummies belonging to the 20th and 21st Dynasties, found in great disorder, in the final chamber of the Tomb.

scattered some of them throughout the corridors in an attempt to give themselves more room in which to work and also to move them towards the limited amount of light which entered the tomb from the shaft and through the small door.

It is ironic that, although Brugsch was a skilled photographer, no photographs were taken of the tomb or the contents. There was simply not time to transport the bulky photographic equipment.

Nicholas Reeves has reconstructed a possible plan of the layout of the tomb at the time of the discovery, based upon scanty reports and notes written soon after the event. The details above are taken from his book *The Valley of the Kings*.

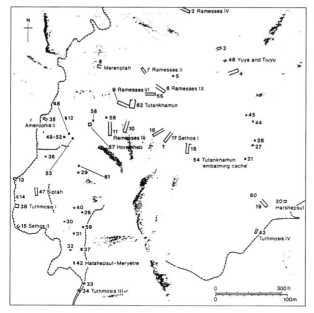

Note:-

KV 35. Tomb of
Amenhotep II.
KV 46. Tomb of Yuya
and Thuya
KV 54. The embalming
cache of Tutankhamun.
KV 55. The so-called
'Tomb of Queen Tiye'.
KV 60. Anonymous Tomb
KV 62. Tomb of
Tutankhamun.

Map of the Valley of the Kings (Fig. 4)

The second discovery of Royal mummies was made in 1898, in the Valley of the Kings. Victor Loret had been excavating there for a while and had just discovered the plundered tomb of Thutmose III. Another tomb, also plundered in antiquity, was found which belonged to Amenhotep II of the Eighteenth Dynasty. Amenhotep was the son of Thutmose III.

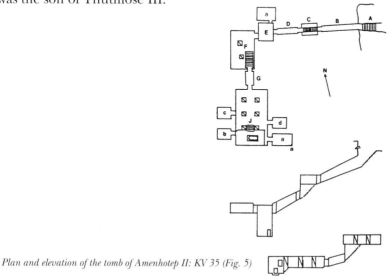

Plan and elevation of the tomb of Amenhotep II: KV 35 (Fig. 5)

17

Smashed items of funerary equipment littered the floor of the tomb of Amenhotep II. The large sarcophagus lay open and to Loret's great surprise it contained a coffin. A bunch of flowers had been placed at the head of the mummy and a wreath of leaves lay at the feet. It was the mummy of Amenhotep II, not in his original coffin, but at least still in his own tomb - the first Pharaoh to be found in the place he had been laid to rest.

In two partly walled-up side chambers to the right of the sarcophagus were found two groups of mummies.

The first chamber (Jc on the plan) contained three uncoffined mummies, two female and one male (although one of the female mummies was initially mistaken for a male).

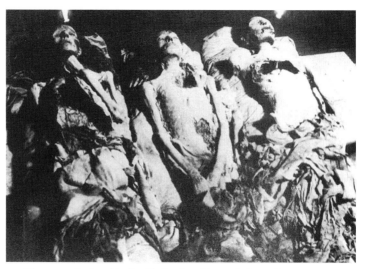

Three mummies found in the side chamber of the tomb of Amenhotep II (Fig. 6)

From the method of embalming used, it is possible that these mummies date to the end of the Eighteenth Dynasty and they may have been originally buried in this tomb. This chamber still holds these mummies and has once again been re-sealed.

The second chamber (Jb on the plan) was still mostly sealed by large limestone blocks. Looking in, Loret could see nine coffins on the floor of the tomb. For the time being this chamber was ignored. Loret spent some time clearing the contents from the rest of the tomb and was still conducting a similar exercise in the tomb of Thutmose III. Only when this work was complete did he turn his attentions to the sealed chamber. He was convinced that the mummies in the chamber would be of minor members of the family of Amenhotep II. The limestone blocks were removed and the coffins revealed. They were all covered by a thick layer of dust and it was not until Loret brushed this away that he was able to read some of the names painted on the coffins. He was as amazed as Brugsch had been to find it was a second Cache of Royal mummies. He read the names which included those of Ramesses IV, Siptah, Seti II and Thutmose IV.

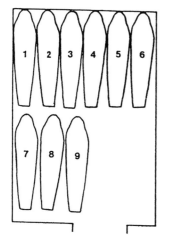

Plan of the side Chamber (Jb) in the tomb of Amenhotep II (Fig. 7)

1. *Thutmose IV.*
2. *Amenhotep III (coffin box of Ramesses III, lid of Seti II).*
3. *Seti II.*
4. *Merneptah (coffin box of Setnakht)*
5. *Siptah.*
6. *Ramesses V.*
7. *Unknown Woman (coffin lid of Setnakht).*
8. *Ramesses VI.*
9. *Ramesses IV.*

Inscriptions on the coffins indicated that they had been moved and re-buried in this tomb at the same time and under similar circumstances, as those found in the first Cache. This second find meant that the mummies of virtually all the Pharaohs of the New Kingdom were now accounted for.

The mummies from the tomb of Amenhotep II were moved to Cairo, with the exception of the mummy of Amenhotep himself, who for a short while was left in his sarcophagus in his tomb. It was not until the tomb was robbed again and some objects stolen from the tomb, that Amenhotep was moved to the safety of the Cairo Museum to join his fellow Pharaohs.

Loret did not keep particularly good records of his excavations and none of the coffins found in the side chamber can be placed with any certainty. Loret does, however, in his published report, list the occupants of the chamber, but they are not listed in chronological order, as might be expected.

Nicholas Reeves suggests that this list may reflect the position of the coffins as they lay in the chamber as they were discovered. The above plan and list of mummies is taken from his book *The Valley of the Kings.*

From the evidence contained in these tombs, inscriptions on the coffins and writings on the bandages of the bodies, it was apparent that the mummies had been hidden at these sites by priests of the Twenty-First Dynasty.

The Royal tombs had obviously suffered a succession of major tomb robberies. Most of the items of any value originally buried in these tombs had been stolen, the mummies alone survived, stripped of their personal jewellery and separated from their original coffins. In many cases the bodies had been hacked to pieces by the robbers in their attempt to obtain all the items of value.

That the Royal mummies should survive at all is nothing short of a miracle, for we know from written accounts of the trials of ancient tomb robbers, that the bodies were often burnt or destroyed.

The surviving Royal mummies were collected by the priests, patched up where necessary, re-wrapped in fine linen, re-coffined and then re-buried, no doubt all amidst great secrecy, in one last desperate attempt to preserve the bodies of some of Egypt's greatest rulers and their families.

Some of the mummies were provided with new coffins, presumably as the originals had been destroyed or were too damaged to use. Hieratic notes written by the priests on coffins and bandages recorded the names of the individuals and a record of the re-wrapping and re-burial. A few of these mummies were moved to several different locations before they reached their final resting place.

When the re-discovered mummies reached Cairo, many were unwrapped and examined immediately by Sir Gaston Maspero. During the early years of this century, a fuller examination was made by Grafton Elliot Smith (1871-1937 A.D.) when most of the remaining wrapped mummies were unwrapped.

The mummy of Thutmose III was the first to be unwrapped, a process which was rushed and unskilled. The mummy was found to have been badly damaged by tomb robbers and this initially discouraged Maspero from unwrapping any other mummies, fearing that they would all be in such a poor state. Eventually Maspero arranged for a group of mummies to be unwrapped in the presence of many modern illustrious personages. By standards established today, the unwrappings were unscientific and fast. The features of Ramesses II were revealed to a modern world in a process which took less than a quarter of one hour.

A visual examination only was possible at this time and detailed measurements were taken and notes made on the appearance of the mummies.

The results of this study were published in 1912 in a large volume entitled *The Royal Mummies*, one of the series of the "Catalogue Général des Antiquitiés Egyptiennes du Musée du Caire".

This volume contains over one hundred excellent black and white photographic plates of the mummies.

The photographs were taken by Emile Brugsch. Each plate was specially prepared for the catalogue and any distracting 'background' was removed from the picture to leave a clear view of the mummy.

These plates are still reproduced today in new publications as they are quite often the only available photographs of some of the mummies.

In addition to his visual examination, Elliot Smith was able to arrange for the mummy of Thutmose IV to be X-Rayed. He realised the great potential of this technique and expressed the wish that in time all the mummies would be examined this way. X-Rays can reveal much detail and can help to put an age to the bodies at the time of death. (This is difficult, if not impossible with a simple visual examination).

A few other mummies have been added to the collections of the Cairo Museum during the course of the last one hundred years.

The most notable discovery is, of course, the tomb of Tutankhamun, discovered in 1922. The mummy of Tutankhamun was left in his tomb, where it still remains today, enclosed in one of his original coffins.

It was a long time before Elliot Smith's wish that the mummies would be the subject of an X-Ray examination was fulfilled. It was not until portable X-Ray equipment was available that the first full examination was made by a team from the University of Michigan in 1966.

Certain restrictions were placed on the team, in that the mummies were not allowed to be removed from their modern coffins and all the work had to be done in the Cairo Museum. Nevertheless, much new and valuable information was obtained during the survey. The results were published in a 'popular' book *X-Raying the Pharaohs* by James E. Harris and Kent R. Weeks and also in a more technical volume *An X-Ray Atlas of the Pharaohs*.

Soon after this examination of the Royal mummies, the mummy of Ramesses II was subjected to a far more scientific and detailed examination, this time outside Egypt, when the mummy was taken to Paris. It had been discovered that the body had begun to deteriorate in the Museum and was in rapid need of conservation. Once again, much was learnt from this study, but apart from some hair, the French were not allowed to take any tissue samples from the body. The results of this work were published in a large, fully illustrated volume entitled *La Momie de Ramses II*.

Other independent research in recent years has enabled two previously unidentified mummies to be identified; those of Queen Tetisheri and Queen Tiye.

All of these examinations, whilst answering some questions, have tended to pose even more. Some mummies are still unidentified and others have had serious doubts cast upon their identifications when, for example, their age as revealed by X-Ray differs radically from the age expected from the historical records. It is more than likely that the priests, in their haste to re-bury the mummies, wrongly identified some of them. This is, in fact, hardly surprising. Imagine one small batch of mummies - five mummies, five coffins. During a robbery, all the mummies could have been removed from their coffins and any objects on the bodies which might give a clue to the identity could have been stolen. We now have five bodies and five coffins, but who can really tell which mummy belongs to which coffin? This is the dilemma the ancient priests undoubtedly faced.

Over the last Century, the ethics of the display of the Royal mummies has often been debated. Elliot Smith was well aware of the problems and in his own introduction to the Catalogue of the mummies stated:-

"In discussing the technique of mummification and the customs associated with it one has to deal with subjects that may possibly give rise to offence, on the ground that it is not showing due respect to the memories of the powerful rulers of Ancient Egypt to display their naked remains and use them as material for anthropological investigations. In fact a good deal of comment has been made in the past in reference to the so called 'sacrilege', on the part of modern archaeologists, in opening the royal tombs and removing and unwrapping the mummies.

Those who make such complaints seem to be unaware that the real desecration was committed twenty-nine centuries ago by the subjects of these rulers; and that modern archaeologists, in doing what they have done, have been rescuing these mummies from the destructive vandalism of the modern descendants of these ancient grave-plunderers".

Certain religious groups in Egypt today still oppose the display of the remains of Egypt's ancient Rulers and the Egyptian Authorities may be unwilling or unable to risk causing local religious dissent.

The Royal mummies have been on public view periodically over the last one hundred years. The Authorities have, from time to time, considered that the remains of Egypt's long dead rulers should not be subjected to public scrutiny. The late President Sadat ordered the mummy room to be closed and wanted the bodies to be returned to their original tombs in the Valley of the Kings. Many eminent Egyptologists were able to convince the President that the mummies were far safer in the Cairo Museum, but the mummy room remained closed.

Some mummies have now been put back back on display. New display cases for the mummies have been designed by the Getty Conservation Institute.

The cases are specially designed to control the climate within the case, which is essential for the preservation of organic materials. The cases are filled with a nitrogen rich atmosphere to re-create the atmosphere in the tombs. Various devices monitor temperature, humidity and changes in air pressure. The result is an environment where bacteria and micro organisms cannot exist. With the mummies sealed in their cases, the worries about damage because of modern pollution and fluctuations in temperature will have been removed and the long-term survival of this unique collection will, hopefully, be assured.

The mummies which will be removed from display will, presumably, be placed in storage, along with other mummies which have never been on display. Some concern must be expressed about the future of these, for it is important that the whole collection be looked after.

Various plans are being drawn up for new Museums to house the enormous collections in the Cairo Museum, so it must be hoped that as much attention is given to the reserve collections as to the objects which will be on display.

A full scientific examination of the Royal mummies has still not been arranged. A team from Manchester Museum, led by Dr. Rosalie David, was asked to conduct such an examination in Cairo a few years ago, but for various reasons this has been delayed and no new dates have as yet been agreed. The results of such an investigation could be far reaching for if the Cairo Museum will allow some tissue samples (and only very small samples are needed) it is possible to be able to ascertain blood groups and to even extract DNA. Once and for all, this could resolve the more doubtful identification of some of the mummies and shed a great deal of light on the family relationships of the Royal families. Such an examination is also likely to pose even more questions, but it is now even more unlikely that any further examination will ever take place. Thirteen of the Royal mummies were X-Rayed again in February 1992. Some of the earlier X-Rays were not clear and this was the last chance before the mummies were sealed in their new display cases. Once sealed, the cases are unlikely to be opened again unless there is considered to be a very important reason to do so.

It is a memorable experience to be able to look into the faces of Egypt's greatest Pharaohs, something the author was able to do in 1980 (but not in 1985 or on subsequent visits, as the mummies had been removed from public display).

In the meantime, the photographs of the mummies in Elliot Smith's Catalogue, and in the accounts of the discovery of other tombs, are the nearest most will get to this experience.

The written accounts and the photographs are, therefore, most important, for it is quite likely that some of the mummies in Cairo may never be seen by the public for a long time, if ever again.

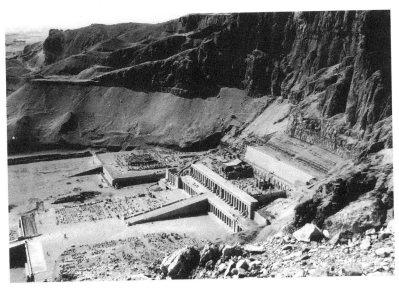

The temples of Hatshepsut and Mentuhotep at Deir el Bahri (Fig. 8)

It was high in the cliffs beyond Hatshepsut's Temple that the tomb containing the First Royal Cache was discovered in 1881

THE ROYAL COFFINS

Interest in the discovery of the Royal mummies at Deir el Bahri was great and Maspero soon published two books.

The first, published in 1881, described briefly the actual discovery and included many photographs of the coffins and other items from the tomb. The photographs are sepia coloured and are mounted on stiff card. The mummies of Thutmose I and Nebseni are shown partly unwrapped to reveal their faces. Identification of the mummies was based on the names on the coffins and wrappings and some of these identifications were proved to be wrong when the mummies were actually unwrapped. The second book was a more detailed work which included photographs of the unwrapped mummies.

The Cairo Museum Catalogue of the coffins was not published until 1909, by which time the collection of Royal mummies had increased, with the discovery of the second Cache in the tomb of Amenhotep II.

The volume of the Catalogue entitled *Cercueils des Cachettes Royales*, was written by M. Georges Daressy. Emile Brugsch provided the superb large black and white photographic plates. The volume included detailed descriptions and measurements of the coffins and copies of the funerary texts (but no translations).

It is clear that when the Royal mummies were re-buried in most cases none of their original coffins had survived, and that other coffins were pressed into service to contain the mummies.

We know, from the magnificent set of coffins which contained the mummy of Tutankhamun, how elaborate the Royal coffins could be and how valuable, in terms of the precious metals used in their construction. It is accepted by most Egyptologists that Tutankhamun's coffins were particularly splendid as he may have fallen heir to funerary items made for two previous Pharaohs (Akhenaten and Smenkhkare) who had rejected some of the funerary beliefs and practices. Tutankhamun also ruled at a time when Egypt was particularly wealthy, with tribute coming in from a large Empire. Tutankhamun's coffins overshadow somewhat the other Royal coffins, but comparison is useful as it can show the evolution of designs, or even the exact opposite - the use of traditional designs for Royal burials.

It is not unreasonable to assume that Pharaohs such as Thutmose III, Amenhotep III and Ramesses II would have had opulent burials too. All of these Kings ruled over a vast and wealthy Empire and reigned far longer than Tutankhamun.

Robbers undoubtedly accounted for much loss. Initially the smaller items would be taken, but if the robberies were not detected the larger items would be plundered too. Gold, whilst always plentiful in Egypt, was much easier to obtain by tomb robbing than by mining and there must have been a considerable amount of re-cycling of the precious metal.

Eventually, the robbed tombs were systematically cleared and any remaining items of value removed. Presumably all the gold items were melted down, but some items such as ushabti and some vessels were re-used for other burials.

The value of the burial equipment which must have lain in the Valley of the Kings at any one time, even if it was all of inferior quality to the equipment of Tutankhamun, must have been enormous and an almost irresistible temptation to robbers.

The earliest tombs in the Valley were designed to be secret and their entrances were concealed.

Later tombs had great entrances and only a sealed door blocked the tomb. It is hard to imagine how any of the tombs could really have been secret. The amount of rock excavated would have been difficult to hide as it would have been a completely different colour from the weathered rock when first excavated. In fact such newly excavated rock might take hundreds of years to weather and mellow. Removal of all the debris from the Valley was probably not possible. Apart from this, there would have been a large number of workmen and officials who would be aware both of the location of the tomb and its contents.

Whilst the Valley may well have been guarded, human nature and greed must have played an important part and it is likely that those who were supposed to protect the burials were probably responsible for plundering some of the tombs. In times of economic crisis, it is not unreasonable to assume that even the King would not have been averse to such re-cycling of wealth.

Gold-covered objects which were not re-used had the gold removed from them. Many of the surviving coffins have had the gold chipped from them, even though this would have been a time-consuming business. The fastest way would be to break the objects into pieces for transportation and later to burn the wood. The gold could then easily be collected. Any solid gold objects could be melted down and then used for making new items. There is evidence in some of the Royal tombs of this activity. Many objects would no doubt have been removed from the Valley and stripped at leisure.

Wood was always a valuable commodity, especially the fine woods such as sycamore and cedar used for quality coffins, so it is likely that those coffins where the outer layer of gold had been removed were re-carved, re-decorated and re-used, not necessarily for other Royal burials. Even coffins recovered intact would need only minor changes to be made for them to be re-used. Once re-used, those tombs too were robbed and the coffins either re-cycled once again or finally destroyed.

With one or two exceptions, the coffins used for the re-burials are of inferior workmanship and have been badly damaged by both ancient, and possibly modern, tomb robbers. Because the majority of the coffins are not considered to be great works of art, only a few are on display in the Cairo Museum today. Few photographs of the coffins are seen in publications today.

In the following pages, the coffins and their mummies have been re-united in photographic form.

It should be noted that the faces of the coffins are not portraits of their occupants, nor were they intended to be. The faces of Tutankhamun's coffins come closest to being portraits, but even these are very stylised.

The 'numbering' of multiple sets of coffins for Tutankhamun and Queen Meryetamun is from the mummy outwards. Thus the coffin nearest the mummy is the first. All the other multiple sets of coffins are numbered from the first coffin encountered inwards. There appears to be no standard convention for this and both systems appear in other publications.

Cairo Museum Catalogue and Exhibition Numbers are quoted for both mummies and coffins.

·Tombs mentioned in the following chapters are referred to by the modern system of numbering, e.g. KV55 (Kings Valley tomb number 55).

THE MUMMIES AND COFFINS

QUEEN TETISHERI.   17th Dynasty.   c.1630 B.C.

Towards the end of the 17th Dynasty, the ruling Theban family began a movement to unite the whole of the Country under their rule. Queen Tetisheri was the wife of Senakhtenre. Both from a non-Royal family, they were to found one of the most powerful lines of rulers Egypt has ever known.

Tetisheri outlived her husband for several years and she, in particular, was heralded as the mother of the line of the New Kingdom Pharaohs. Original tomb unknown.

The Mummy: Found in the Royal Cache at Deir el Bahri, in 1881.
Cairo Museum Catalogue Number **61056.**

The mummy, now believed to be that of Queen Tetisheri, was found in a coffin bearing the names of Ramesses I. It was not until the body was fully unwrapped that it was realised it was female.

Elliot Smith dated the mummy to the 17th Dynasty, by the mummification techniques used, which were typical of the period, but he was unable to identify the body which was simply known as 'unknown woman **B**'.

The mummy, like many of the other Royal bodies, had been badly damaged by the tomb-robbers when stripping it of the jewellery it once wore. This unknown woman was obviously quite old when she died; she was noticeably bald and her own white hair was interwoven with artificial braids.

The head, broken from the body, was the first to be examined by the Michigan team. The X-Rays showed the same shape of skull seen in four generations of the early New Kingdom mummies, particularly the women. This fact alone pointed to the identification of the mummy as that of Queen Tetisheri. She had moderately worn teeth and an impacted third molar tooth which lay at an unusual angle in the jaw and marked maxillary protrusion (buck teeth). All these dental features are seen in her descendants.

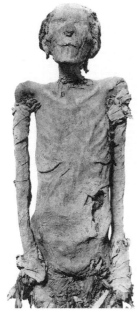

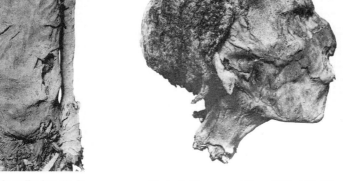

The mummy of Queen Tetisheri (Fig 9)　　　　*The head of the mummy of Queen Tetisheri (Fig 10)*

Height of the body, 1.570 Metres.

The Coffin:　　Cairo Museum Catalogue Number **61018**.

The coffin which contained Queen Tetisheri was probably made in the 21st Dynasty, when the Royal mummies were re-buried. Made of sycamore, it was probably not made especially for the re-burial, but was 'pressed' into service. A hole in the forehead of the coffin shows where an Uraeus was once placed to indicate a Royal occupant, but this has not survived.

The wood of the coffin has been covered in a layer of plaster which has been painted and gilded. Little of the gilding survives and the surface of the coffin has been badly damaged by the tomb-robbers. The priests of the 21st Dynasty were clearly under the impression that the body they were placing in this coffin was that of Ramesses I and it was his name they wrote on the coffin. This mistake is probably indicative of the great damage to the original burials and the speed with which they had to work.

The mummy of Ramesses I has not yet been found (or identified).

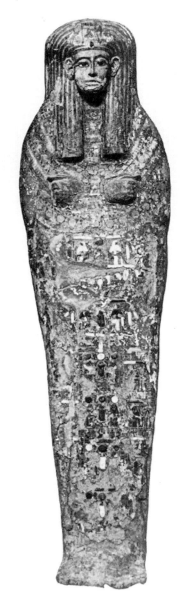

The lid of the coffin of Queen Tetisheri / Ramesses I (Fig 11)

Length of the coffin, 1.92 metres. Breadth, 0.52 metres.

SEQUENENRE-TAO II   17th Dynasty.   c. 1574 B.C.

It was under Sequenenre-Tao, son of Senakhtenre-Tao and Queen Tetisheri, that the struggle to expel the Hyksos began, in an attempt to re-unite Egypt under one rule. Original tomb unknown.

The Mummy: Found in the Royal Cache at Deir el Bahri in 1881.
Cairo Museum Catalogue Number **61051**.
Exhibition Number **6342**.

The mummy of Sequenenre was unrolled by Maspero on June 9th 1886 and the few wrappings left on the limbs were removed by Elliot Smith in 1906 .

All that remains of this King is a very badly damaged, disarticulated skeleton. An early engraving of the mummy, taken before the examination by Elliot Smith, does show a more recognisable body. Clearly the final unwrapping damaged further an already damaged body.

The soft tissue which remains is moist, dark brown and still pliable, with a strongly aromatic spicy odour, noted by Elliot Smith.

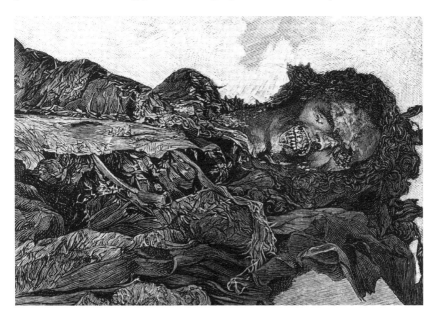

The mummy of Sequenenre-Tao: An engraving which was made before 1888 (Fig 12)

31

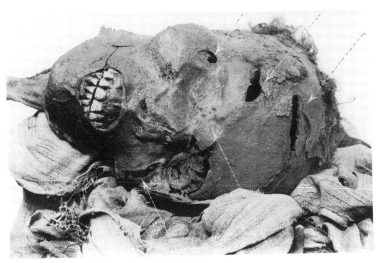

The head of the mummy of Sequenenre-Tao (Fig 13)

The Michigan team also commented on this smell when they examined the mummy, although they described it as a "..strong odour, a rather foul, oily smell", which filled the room when the display case in the Museum was opened. Elliot Smith attributed this smell to aromatic sawdust which had been sprinkled over the body. It was, however, also evident that the body had been badly embalmed.

Sequenenre clearly met a very violent death and the embalmers made no attempt to straighten the body out into the customary position. This lack of proper embalming is taken as evidence that he was mummified away from his City of Thebes and the embalmers workshops. Maspero suggested that he died and was badly embalmed on the field of battle.

Five wounds are found on the head. Elliot Smith describes two axe cuts, which both fractured the skull on the forehead; a blow with a 'blunt instrument', to the bridge of the nose; a further blow with a sharp instrument, to the left cheek and a similar wound to the right side of the head.

Elliot Smith surmised that Sequenenre met his death in an attack by two or more persons, with at least two types of weapon; an axe and spears or arrows.

There are no traces of wounds to any other parts of the body, so Sequenenre was clearly unable to offer any resistance to the blows. In most situations, the arms would have been used to defend the head, but they are unmarked.

The nature of the axe wounds indicates that the King was lying on his right side when he was hit, either felled by one of the other blows and then hit again when he was prostrate, or even attacked when he was asleep. He ruled in troubled times, so either is possible; we shall probably never know the answer.

Elliot Smith estimated the King's age at death to be between thirty and forty. The Michigan team established his age at about thirty.

After the injuries were received, death must have been instant or at least soon after death. If the King had survived any length of time the X-Rays would have revealed new bone formation and healing.

In life, Sequenenre would have been slender and muscular with a small, long, barrel-shaped head, covered with long black curly hair. He possesses a remarkably healthy set of teeth, which is not a particularly common attribute of an Egyptian Pharaoh.

Various Scholars have in the past suggested a Nubian origin for Sequenenre and his family and his facial features do suggest that this may be true.

The Coffin: Cairo Museum Catalogue Number **61001.**
                       Exhibition Number **3893.**

Sequenenre was found in a large anthropoid cedar wood coffin, which was probably the one in which he was originally buried.

The King is shown wearing the usual Nemes head-dress. An Uraeus originally reared its head above the brow of the King, but now only the body of the snake remains.

The surface of the coffin is painted yellow, although it was once covered by a layer of white plaster which was then gilded. A feather design was originally engraved over the body of the coffin. Known as 'rishi', this design is a common feature of Royal coffins.

Little of the gilding remains; this was probably removed by tomb-robbers, but whether anciently or in more recent times, is not known.

The robbers were certainly very patient, for they carefully scraped the gold from the coffin and concealed the patches they laid bare with yellow paint.

Some areas were left gilded, such as the Royal Insignia and it has been argued that such devoutly inspired discrimination would only have been shown by the priests, presumably those responsible for the re-burials.

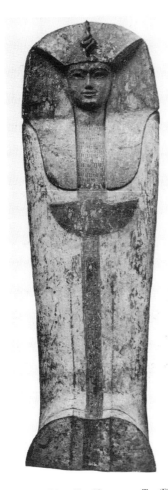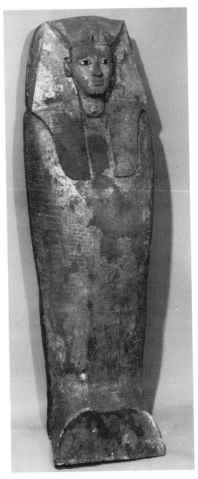

The lid of the coffin of Sequenenre -Tao (Fig 14) *The coffin of Inyotef V in the British Museum (Fig 15)*

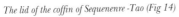

The design of the coffin is almost identical to others which survive from the 17th Dynasty. The coffin of Inyotef V is in the British Museum and shows the typically large head-dress and the remains of the gilded feather design.

The King would probably have been buried with a set of two or three coffins, but only this one has survived.

Length of coffin 2.12 Metres. Breadth 0.70 metres.
Height 0.53 metres.

QUEEN AHOTEP I.   17th Dynasty.   c.1600 B.C.

Queen Ahotep was the daughter of Senakhtenre-Tao I and Queen Tetisheri, sister and wife of Sequenenre-Tao II and mother of Ahmose I. The location of her original tomb is unknown.

The Coffin: Found in the Royal Cache at Deir el Bahri in 1881.
Cairo Museum Catalogue Number **61006.**
Exhibition Number **3888.**

The huge coffin of Queen Ahotep was found to contain the coffin of Pinudjem I, of the 21st Dynasty.

Presumably this coffin was originally used for the burial of Queen Ahotep, but had become separated from the mummy, which was found in 1859 in a small tomb near the entrance to the Valley of the Kings. Details of this discovery are vague and the coffin containing the mummy changed hands several times. Several items of jewellery were discovered on the mummy, which was probably the first significant find of this kind. The mummy was considered unimportant and was probably discarded or destroyed. The coffin and the pieces of jewellery eventually found their way into the Cairo Museum (where they were some of the first exhibits). The coffin (which is not illustrated here) is similar in design to the inner coffin of Queen Meryet-Amun, but substantially more intact, with the gold overlay surviving.

The coffin illustrated here is probably the second of an original set of three prepared for the Queen and is virtually identical to the coffin of Queen Ahmose-Nefertari, also discovered in the same Cache (see page 57).

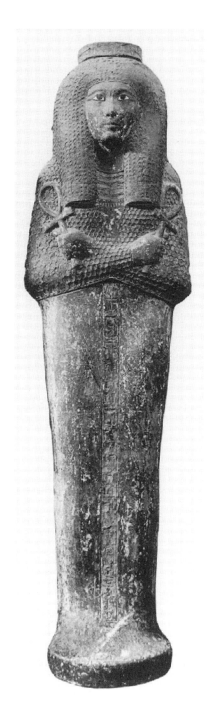

The lid of the coffin of Queen Ahotep I (Fig 16)

Now somewhat battered, the coffin would have originally been covered by a thin layer of plaster and gilded.

The upper half of the coffin was inlaid with coloured scales of glass paste. The lower part was incised with the usual feather 'rishi' design.

None of the inlay remains and virtually all of the gold has been lost. An inscription running down the centre of the coffin lid gives the names and titles of the Queen.

The crossed hands of the coffin each hold a symbol of life, the Ankh.

On top of the heavy wig is the base of a crown. Two carved wooden plumes would have once surmounted the crown, but these are now missing. When complete it would have looked similar to the crown on the coffin of Queen Ahmose-Nefertari. (See page 57)

Length of the coffin 3.12 metres. Breadth 0.98 metres. Height 0.63 metres.

QUEEN AHMOSE - INHAPI.   17th Dynasty.   c. 1600 B.C.

Ahmose-Inhapi was a daughter of Senakhtenre-Tao I and the wife of Sequenenre-Tao II. The location of her original tomb is not known.

The Mummy: Found in the Royal Cache at Deir el Bahri in 1881.
Cairo Museum Catalogue Number **61053**.

The mummy of Ahmose-Inhapi was unwrapped in 1886. Restored by the priests of the 21st Dynasty, the wrapped mummy was garlanded with flowers.

The bandages were extremely dry and powdery to the touch. When revealed, the body was found to be that of a strongly built woman arranged in the usual female position with her hands extended by her thighs.

The state of preservation of the mummy is poor, with the skin being dark brown, moist, tough and soft like oiled leather. From the embalming techniques Elliot Smith dated the mummy to the early New Kingdom.

The head of the Queen is covered with dark hair arranged in 'wheat ear' like plaits which have been smeared with resinous paste.

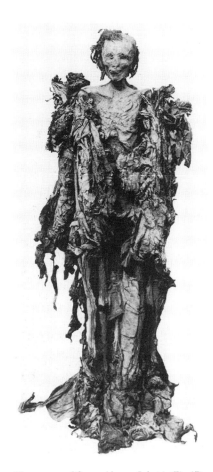

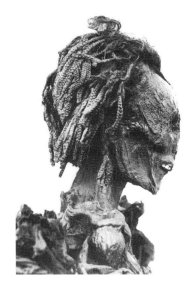

The mummy of Queen Ahmose-Inhapi (Fig 17)

*The head of the mummy of
Queen Ahmose-Inhapi (Fig 18)*

The pressure of the bandages has distorted the features of the face.

The photograph of the mummy illustrates well the rushed and unscientific manner of the unwrapping in the Cairo Museum.

In recent examinations and unwrappings of mummies, the bandages have been removed one layer at a time and subject to detailed examination, which can reveal much additional information. Here the bandages have been simply cut through to reveal the body as quickly as possible.

Height of the body 1.685 metres.

38

The Coffin: Cairo Museum Catalogue Number **61004.**

The mummy of Queen Ahmose-Inhapi was found in a coffin belonging to the Lady Rai. (The mummy of Rai was also found in the Deir el Bahri Cache, in another coffin).

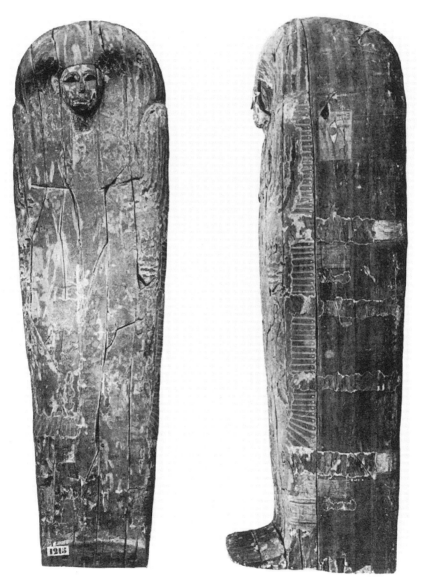

The coffin of Queen Ahmose-Inhapi /Rai (Fig 19)

Made of sycamore and acacia, this coffin is probably the original outer coffin of Rai.

Typically late 17th early 18th Dynasty in design, the wig is very large in proportion to the rest of the coffin.

The coffin has been greatly damaged by robbers and hardly any of the original decoration survives. Any gilding which may have covered parts of the coffin has been hacked away.

The inlaid eyes of the coffin have been stolen.

Some traces of a painted feather design remain outlined in yellow with a background of blue and white.

Length of the coffin 2.39 metres. Breadth 0.74 metres. Height 0.70 metres.

AHMOSE-HENTEMPET.   17th Dynasty.   c. 1580 B. C.

Ahmose-Hentempet was the daughter of Sequenenre-Tao II and Queen Ahotep. The location of her original tomb is not known.

The Mummy: Found in the Royal Cache at Deir el Bahri in 1881.
Cairo Museum Catalogue Number **61062**.

When discovered, this mummy was superficially intact, although a hole had been made in the bandages of the chest.

When unwrapped, a badly damaged mummy was revealed. Both forearms have been broken off; only fragments of the right remain and the detached left forearm has been placed across the body.

The linen packing of the nostrils has been forced out by the pressure of the bandages, giving the mummy a somewhat gruesome appearance.

The head is covered in thick dark hair. A large wig was found placed on the chest of the mummy and enclosed within the wrappings. It had, presumably, been placed there by the restorers of the burial. It is not known if this wig was part of the original burial of Ahmose-Hentempet.

Length of the body 1.613 metres.

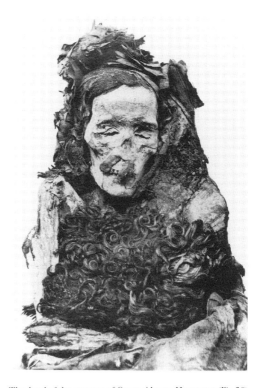

The head of the mummy of Queen Ahmose-Hentempet (Fig 20)

The Coffin: Cairo Museum Catalogue Number **61017.**

Ahmose-Hentempet was found in an 18th Dynasty coffin which replaced her (presumably lost or too damaged to use) original.

Made of sycamore, the coffin is painted black, apart from the eyes which have been detailed in white.

The name of the original owner of the coffin has been erased and the name of Ahmose-Hentempet substituted.

Length of the coffin 2.0 metres. Breadth 0.50 metres.
Height 0.68 metres.

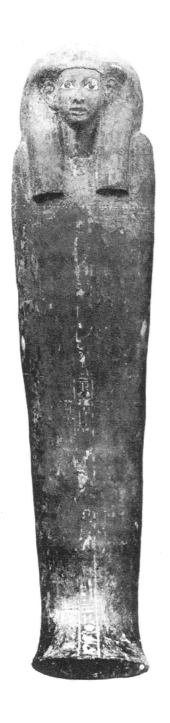

The coffin of Queen Ahmose-Hentempet (Fig 21)

AHMOSE-HETTIMEHU.   17th Dynasty.   c. 1575 B.C.

Ahmose-Hettimehu was the daughter of Sequenenre-Tao II and Queen Ahmose-Inhapi. The location of her original tomb is not known.

The Mummy: Found in the Royal Cache at Deir el Bahri in 1881. Cairo Museum Catalogue Number **61061.**

Before unwrapping, this mummy appeared to be intact. It soon became clear, when the wrappings were removed, that the priests had re-wrapped a damaged mummy whose original wrappings had been hacked to pieces by robbers to reach the jewellery on the body.

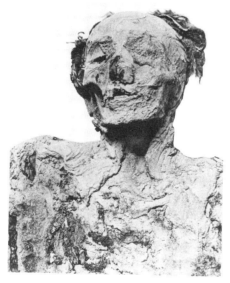

The head of the mummy of Ahmose-Hettimehu (Fig 22)

The surviving original bandages were powdery and brittle to the touch.

Some dark hair remains on the head, which is still covered in places by a layer of resin and solidified bandages.

Areas of soft tissue have been lost, probably when the body was badly handled by the robbers. Plugs of linen and resin closed the nostrils and can clearly be seen.

Height of the body 1.520 metres.

The Coffin: Cairo Museum Catalogue Number **61012.**

The mummy of Ahmose-Hettimehu was found in a badly damaged coffin of early 18th Dynasty date.

Made of acacia and now painted white, the coffin was originally covered in gold which has been stripped away by robbers.

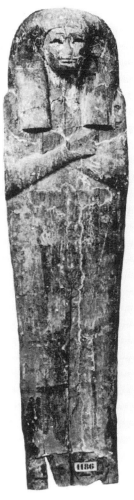

The lid of the coffin of Ahmose-Hettimehu (Fig 23)

The face has been severely mutilated and the inlaid eyes hacked out.

Length of the coffin 2.0 metres. Breadth 0.56 metres. Height 0.57 metres.

AHMOSE.   18th Dynasty.   1570-1546 B.C.

It was Ahmose, founder of the 18th Dynasty, who finally drove the Hyksos from Egypt and re-united the Country under a single ruler. By doing so, he also re-established the supremacy of Thebes. Ahmose was the son of Sequenenre-Tao and Queen Ahotep. Original tomb unknown.

The Mummy: Found in the Royal Cache at Deir el Bahri, in 1881.
               Cairo Museum Catalogue Number 61057.
               Exhibition Number 6343.

This body's identity was written on the coffin in hieroglyphs and confirmed by an hieratic note written on the bandages. The name of his successor and son, Amenhotep I, who gave the orders for the embalming, was also noted, as was the name of the Priest-King of Thebes, Pinudjem II, of the 21st Dynasty, during whose reign the body was re-wrapped.

The mummy of Ahmose had been broken by tomb robbers, but it had originally been covered in a tough, black resinous paste, which protected it to some extent. This paste did, however, make examination difficult, both for Elliot Smith and the Michigan team.

X-Rays, which were not particularly clear, managed to show that Ahmose probably suffered badly from arthritis in his knees and back, which must have made movement difficult.

These X-Rays also revealed that Ahmose, unlike most Pharaohs, was uncircumcised. He was delicately built and he may have been considered too frail to undergo the operation.

The X-Rays did manage to show that there were strong similarities between the bodies of Ahmose and Sequenenre, confirming a close family link.

The age of Ahmose at death has been estimated to be around forty years.

Height of the body 1.635 metres.

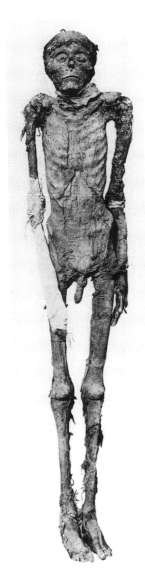

The mummy of Ahmose (Fig 24)

The Coffin: Cairo Museum Catalogue Number **61002.**
Exhibition Number **3894.**

The body of Ahmose was found in a large cedar wood coffin which has been dated to the 18th Dynasty but shows signs of later repairs, possibly during the 21st Dynasty.

As with other coffins which contained the Royal mummies, this coffin was probably not the original and is of a non-Royal type.

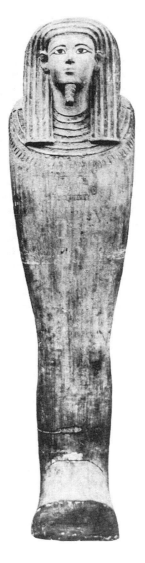

The lid of the coffin of Ahmose (Fig 25)

Although it appears to be well preserved, it too was damaged by the tomb robbers, who removed all the inlay from the collar and wig areas and most of the gold from the body of the coffin. The coffin was covered with a feather design, identical to that seen on the earlier Royal coffins. An inscribed pectoral on the chest of the coffin gives the name and titles of the King.

Length of the coffin 1.78 metres. Breadth 0.48 metres. Height 0.43 metres.

PRINCE SIAMEN.   18th Dynasty.   Date Uncertain.

The Mummy: Found in the Royal Cache at Deir el Bahri in 1881.
Cairo Museum Catalogue Number **61059**.

The mummy of this otherwise unknown Prince was found in an
extremely damaged state. Probably dating to the early part of the
18th Dynasty, the mummy had been hacked apart by robbers. The
restorers of the burial made no attempt to replace the bones of the
skeleton in their proper positions, but simply threw them pell-mell
into an oblong bundle.

Height of the body 0.98 metres.

Note: This mummy is not illustrated.

The Coffin: Cairo Museum Catalogue Number **61008**.

Dating to the 18th Dynasty, this coffin is made of cedar and bears a
marked similarity to the coffin of Ahmose I. The head-dress is
painted in blue and yellow stripes and there are indications that the
yellow paint replaced the original gold which covered the coffin.
The eyes are detailed in black and white paint. No hands are shown
on this coffin.

A broad falcon collar covers the chest of the coffin which was
once inlaid with coloured bands, probably of glass paste or semi-
precious stones, which have now been removed.

The body of the coffin is covered in the 'rishi' feathered
design. An inscription on the feet of the coffin gives the name of the
Prince.

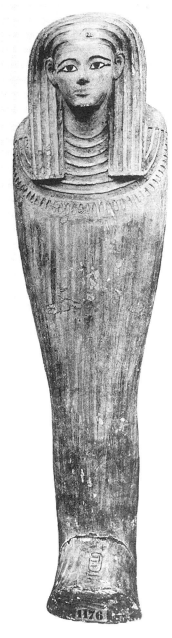

The lid of the coffin of Siamen (Fig 26)

Length of the coffin 1.65 metres. Breadth 0.45 metres.
Height 0.37 metres.

SITKAMOSE.   18th Dynasty.   c.1530 B.C.

As the name implies, Sitkamose was probably a daughter of Kamose. The location of her original tomb is not known.

The Mummy: Found in the Royal Cache at Deir el Bahri in 1881.
Cairo Museum Catalogue Number **61063.**
Exhibition Number **6391.**

The mummy of Sitkamose, garlanded with flowers, was unwrapped by Maspero on June 19th 1886. Maspero discovered that this mummy had been re-wrapped by the priests of the 21st Dynasty at the same time as the mummy of Ahmose.

The body has been subject to severe damage by robbers who chopped through the bandages to reach any objects of value.

The body is of a large woman which has been poorly embalmed.

The whole body is covered in a thick layer of a resinous paste, which is similar to the treatment of the mummy of Ahmose.

An unusual feature for this period is that the hands are extended in front of the pubic area, rather than being laid by the sides.

The head has been damaged, which has revealed that no attempt was made to remove the brains.

The toes bear impressions of the string used to keep the toe nails in place during the process of mummification. The resin coating on other parts of the body retains the impressions of now lost jewellery.

The body cavity is packed with linen, which can be seen through the damaged body wall. The left arm is broken off at the shoulder.

X-Rays taken of the body indicate an age at death of between thirty and thirty-five.

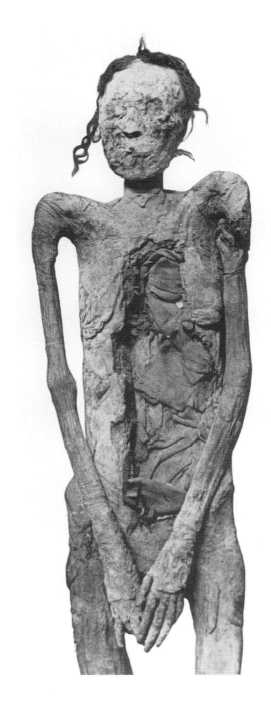

The mummy of Sitkamose (Fig 27)

Height of the body 1.620 metres.

The Coffin: Cairo Museum Catalogue Number **61011.**

The mummy of Sitkamose was found in a 20th or 21st Dynasty coffin inscribed for one Pediamun.

A poor coffin, it is made of sycamore covered in plaster with detailed funerary scenes painted on a yellow background.

The details of the wig are painted in alternate yellow and blue stripes.

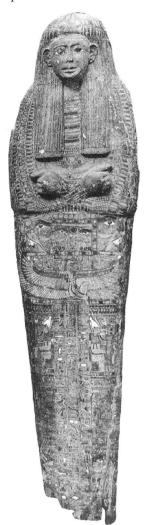

The lid of the coffin of Sitkamose (Fig 28)

Length of the coffin 1.78 metres. Breadth 0.51 metres. Height 0.47 metres.

PRINCE AHMOSE-SIPAIR.   18th Dynasty.   c. 1530 B.C.

Little is known about this Prince, who was a son of Ahmose I.

The Mummy: Found in the Royal Cache at Deir el Bahri in 1881.
              Cairo Museum Catalogue Number **61064.**

The mummy of Prince Ahmose-Sipair is that of a young boy of
uncertain age.

    The body was re-wrapped by restorers and appeared to be
superficially intact. It had, however, been damaged by the
robbers and the priests used a stout stick which was tied to the
mummy and enclosed in the bandages to give the small body some
rigidity. Some of the bones from the body are missing.

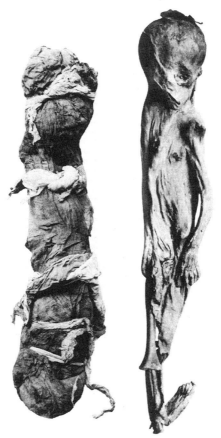

The mummy of Prince Ahmose-Sipair (Fig 29)

The Coffin: Cairo Museum Catalogue Number **61007**.

The body of the Prince was found in a replacement coffin which probably dates to the end of the 18th Dynasty.

It is similar, though much smaller, to the second coffin of Yuya and to the two coffins containing infant burials from the tomb of Tutankhamun.

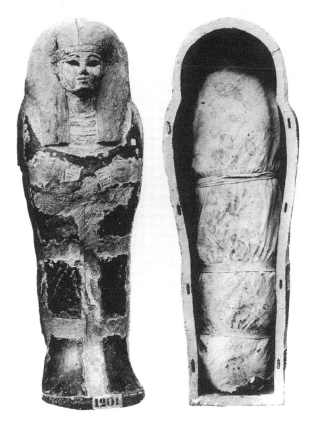

The coffin and wrapped mummy of Prince Ahmose-Sipair (Fig 30)

Made from sycamore, the coffin has been painted with black pitch. The wig, face, hands and the bands running around the coffin were modelled in plaster over the wood and gilded. All the gold has now been stripped from these areas and the inlaid eyes of the coffin have been stolen.

Length of the coffin 1.22 metres. Breadth 0.40 metres.
Height 0.56 metres.

QUEEN AHMOSE-NEFERTARI. 18th Dynasty. c.1550 B.C.

Queen Ahmose-Nefertari was both the sister and wife of Ahmose. In reliefs during the reign of Ahmose, she is shown the same size as the King and the Gods, an unusual mark of distinction. Like her grandmother Tetisheri, her memory was perpetuated after her death.

Original tomb unknown.

The Mummy.   Found in the Royal Cache at Deir el Bahri in 1881.
Cairo Museum Catalogue Number **61055**.
Exhibition Number 6360.

The mummy of Queen Ahmose-Nefertari was unwrapped by Emile Brugsch in 1885. This body too had been damaged by tomb-robbers; the left hand and the right forearm and hand are missing.

A few black resin-coated bandages from the original wrappings remain on the body. Ahmose-Nefertari died at an advanced age, possibly seventy and her body is emaciated.

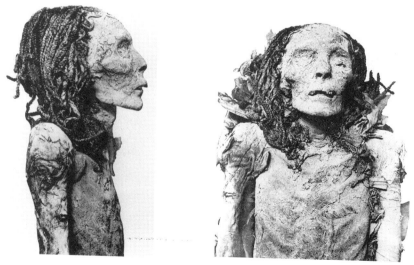

The mummy of Queen Ahmose-Nefertari (Fig 31 and 32)

At the time of her death, the Queen had little of her own hair left. The hair seen on the mummy is false: twenty strings of twisted human hair have been placed across the top of the head, to which have been attached numerous tight plaits of hair, each about thirty centimetres long.

Ahmose-Nefertari exhibits many of the same dental characteristics as her grandmother Tetisheri. The prominent front teeth are, if anything, more pronounced. In addition to the dentition, there is also a marked similarity in skeletal form.

It is interesting to note that the skeleton of Ahmose-Nefertari shows little similarity to that of her brother Ahmose. It is possible, therefore, that while they had the same father, they may have had different mothers.

The Coffin. Cairo Museum Catalogue Number **61003**.
Exhibition Number **3892**.

The body of Queen Ahmose-Nefertari was found in a colossal wooden coffin.

Several examples survive of these coffins which are of a type commonly used for the Queens of the early 18th Dynasty.

The Queen is shown wearing a heavy wig and crown. Her hands are crossed over her chest and the hands hold Ankh symbols.

The top part of the coffin was once inlaid with either semi-precious stones or coloured glass paste. None of this inlay survives and any gilding on the coffin has also been lost.

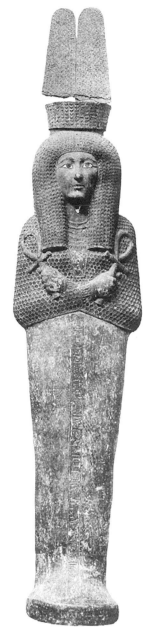

The lid of the coffin of Queen Ahmose-Nefertari (Fig 33)

Length of the coffin, excluding the head-dress 3.78 metres. Breadth 0.82 metres. Height 0.48 metres.

This coffin also contained the mummy of Ramesses III.

THE LADY RAI.   18th Dynasty.   c. 1540 B.C.

The Lady Rai was a wet-nurse of Queen Ahmose-Nefertari and possibly also of Ahmose I. The location of her original tomb is not known.

The Mummy: Found in the Royal Cache at Deir el Bahri in 1881.
Cairo Museum Catalogue Number **61054.**

The mummy of Rai is that of a graceful and delicate woman with well proportioned limbs.

The arms are fully extended with the palms resting on the thighs. Her hands are small and delicate, being almost childlike in appearance.

Linen was used to fill the body cavity and can be seen through the embalming incision in the side of the mummy.

The whole body was sprinkled with a mixture of powdered resin and sand.

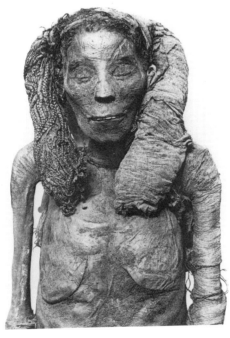 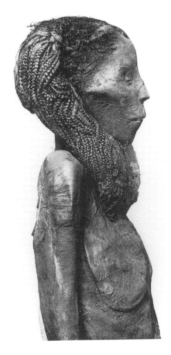

The mummy of Rai (Figs 34 and 35)

Rai has abundant hair, which is arranged in small plaits which are divided into two thick masses arranged on either side of her face. This form of hair-style is well known from statues of this period.

Height of the body 1.510 metres.

The Coffin: Cairo Museum Catalogue Number **61022.**

The mummy of Rai was not found in one of her own original coffins but in a 20th Dynasty coffin inscribed for one Paheripedjet. One of her own coffins actually survived and was included in the Cache at Deir el Bahri, but it had been re-used by the priests for the body of Queen Ahmose-Inhapi.

The body of Rai enclosed in her 'new' coffin, was surrounded by large quantities of linen, presumably placed there by the priests restoring the burials.

Made of sycamore, this coffin has been plastered and painted and is covered in funerary texts. No attempt was made on this occasion to alter the texts or name for the new occupant of the coffin.

The face is painted red with the stripes of the head-dress in yellow and blue.

The arms in raised relief are crossed and the hands hold the symbols of the God Osiris and the Goddess Isis.

The funerary scenes and texts are brightly painted, as is usual for coffins of this period.

The entire surface of the coffin has been given a coating of yellow varnish.

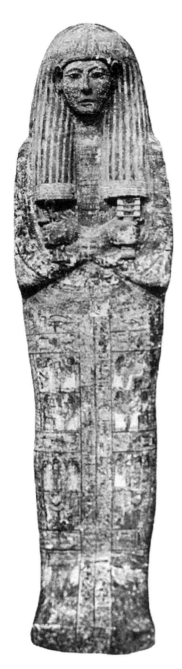

The lid of the coffin of Rai (Fig 36)

Length of the coffin 2.01 metres. Breadth 0.58 metres. Height 0.70 metres.

SITAMUN.   18th Dynasty.   c. 1530 B.C.

Sitamun was the daughter of Ahmose I and Queen Ahmose-Nefertari.

The Mummy: Found in the Royal Cache at Deir el Bahri in 1881.
           Cairo Museum Catalogue Number **61090.**

The mummy of Sitamun, whilst appearing to be superficially intact, when unwrapped proved to be an oblong wrapped bundle, containing bones and reeds thrown together and surmounted by a skull. This body had obviously been hacked to pieces by robbers and no soft tissue remains on the broken and disarticulated skeleton.

Note: This mummy is not illustrated.

The Coffin: Cairo Museum Catalogue Number **61009.**

The mummy of Sitamun was found in a small sycamore anthropoid coffin.

The coffin may well have been used to contain the remains of Sitamun which were no longer in a recognisable human shape.

The wrapped bundle of bones took up less space than an intact extended body.

The coffin is covered in stucco, both inside and out, which has been painted white. Dating to the 18th Dynasty it is devoid of any decoration or inscription.

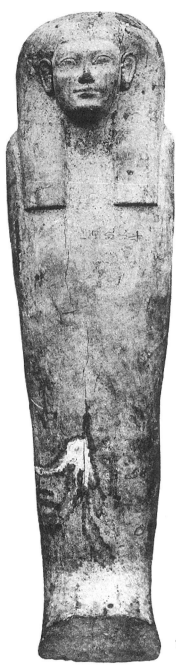

The lid of the coffin of Sitamun.(Fig 37)

Length of the coffin 1.28 metres. Breadth 0.36 metres.
Height 0.33 metres.

AMENHOTEP I.   18th Dynasty.   1551-1524 B.C.

Amenhotep I was the son of Ahmose and Queen Ahmose-Nefertari. After the death of his father, he co-reigned with his mother and they were both later worshipped as Gods. He was a great patron of the Theban God Amun .

Amenhotep was the first Pharaoh to build his tomb and mortuary temple at different sites. His idea must have been to have a secret tomb, for it was probably obvious that earlier Royal burials were being plundered and he intended his burial to remain undisturbed. Sadly, this was not to be the case.

His temple was located on the edge of the cultivated area on the west bank of the river at Thebes; a tomb in the hillside at Dra' Abu el Naga, discovered by Howard Carter in 1914, may belong to Amenhotep.

The Mummy: Found in the Royal Cache at Deir el Bahri in 1881.
Cairo Museum Catalogue Number **61058**.
Exhibition Number **6344**.

The mummy of Amenhotep I was re-wrapped by the priests of the 21st Dynasty. This re-wrapping was done so well that neither Maspero nor Elliot Smith attempted to unwrap the body for fear of damaging the extremely delicate linen.

A funeral mask of cartonnage (linen and plaster) was still in place over the head and the entire body was garlanded with flowers. When the Michigan team removed the lid from the museum case they were greeted with the smell of delphiniums, which still lingered after virtually two and a half thousand years. X-Rays provided the first view inside the wrappings and were the first to be taken of a fully wrapped mummy. The skeleton of the King was clearly revealed. Like his predecessors he had a pronounced chin and protruding front teeth and his teeth showed little dental wear.

Also shown on the X-Rays was a belt of large beads placed around the hips and a small amulet on the right arm, both probably added at the re-wrapping.

Height of the body 1.785 metres.

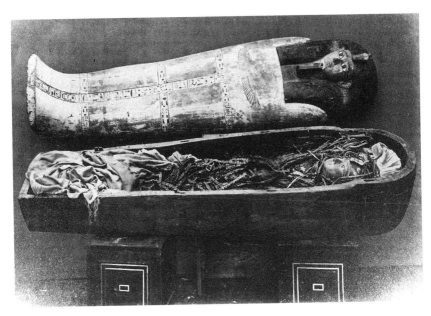

The coffin and wrapped mummy of Amenhotep I (Fig 38)

The Coffin: Cairo Museum Catalogue Number **61005**.
Exhibition Number 3874.

A cedar wood coffin contained the body of Amenhotep I. The coffin has been dated to the 18th Dynasty but is not the one originally used for the King. It is of a non-Royal type and the previous owner has been identified by the remains of inscription as an individual named Thot-nefer, of whom nothing is known.

The face of the coffin is framed by a heavy black wig. The Royal Uraeus has been added to the brow and a beard, now broken away, once adorned the Royal chin. It is interesting to note that the earlier photographs of the coffin do appear to show the beard in place although it is missing from the illustrations in the Catalogue of coffins and from the coffin itself, which is exhibited today in the Cairo Museum.

The face is painted yellow, with the eyes detailed in black and white paint. The paint has been applied over a thin coat of plaster laid over the wood.

A painted yellow band runs down the front of the coffin, with three transverse bands. Black painted hieroglyphs on these bands give the names and titles of the King. The vulture Goddess Nekhbet is shown with wings outstretched on the chest of the coffin. A hieratic note, written above the vulture, was made by the priests at the time of the re-burial.

Length of the coffin 2.03 metres. Breadth 0.57 metres. Height 0.67 metres.

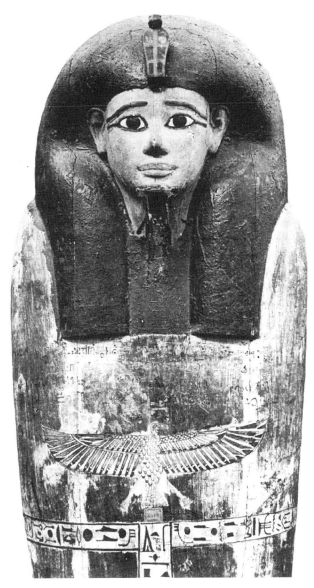

The lid of the coffin of Amenhotep I (detail) (Fig 39)

QUEEN AHMOSE-MERYETAMUN.   18th Dynasty.
                                         Date Uncertain.

The Mummy.   Found in the Royal Cache at Deir el Bahri in 1881.
Cairo Museum Catalogue Number **61052.**

The mummy of Ahmose-Meryetamun, like so many others, has been
badly damaged by robbers. The body wall has been broken which
has revealed the linen packing filling the body cavity. The right arm
of the mummy has been completely broken off and is missing, whilst
only the upper part of the left arm remains.

Height of the body 1.470 metres.

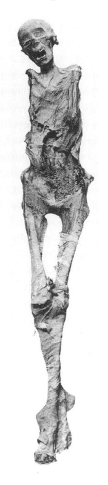

The mummy of Queen Ahmose-Meryetamun (Fig 40)

The Coffin: Cairo Museum Catalogue Number **61010.**

The mummy of Ahmose-Meryetamun was discovered in a 'replacement' coffin which belonged to the Steward Seniu of the 18th Dynasty.

The body of the coffin is painted white with the bands of inscriptions outlined in blue with blue hieroglyphs on a yellow background. The face has had all the decoration hacked away which indicates that it may have been covered in gold, as were the hands.

The wig is blue with yellow lines dividing it into the usual stripes.

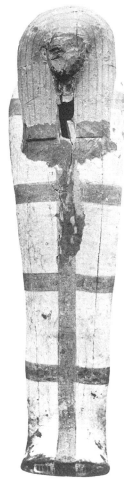

The lid of the coffin of Queen Ahmose-Meryetamun (Fig 41)

Length of the coffin 2.16 metres. Breadth 0.59 metres. Height 0.64 metres.

BAKT.   18th Dynasty.   Date uncertain.

The Mummy: Found in the Royal Cache at Deir el Bahri in 1881.
                Cairo Museum Catalogue Number **61076**.

This wrapped mummy had obviously received the attentions of robbers and had been re-wrapped by the priests of the 21st Dynasty.

The body was garlanded with flowers over the bandages which had been chopped through, revealing the bones of a young woman. Very little soft tissue remains on the body.

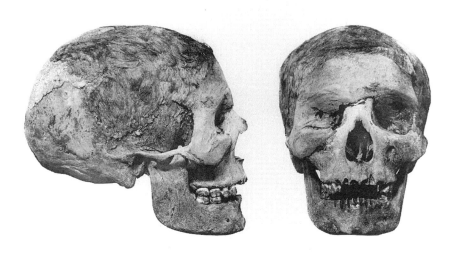

The head of the mummy of Bakt (Fig 42)

Included in the wrappings was a fragment of yellow-varnished coffin and a mirror handle.

The mummy is presumed to be that of Bakt because it was found in a coffin bearing that name. No name was recorded on the wrappings of the mummy and this identification must, therefore, be suspect.

The Coffin: Cairo Museum Catalogue Number **61015.**

The body, presumed to be that of Bakt, was found in a replacement cedar coffin with a face made from sycamore. Dating to the 18th Dynasty, it shows signs of being re-used before Bakt for a Royal mummy whose identity is not known.

The surface has been adzed over which indicates it must once have been covered in gold. The inlaid eyes have been removed. The head-dress is painted blue and an inscription in black remains on the coffin. This inscription has been mostly washed or worn away and is now very difficult to read.

Length of the coffin 2.0 metres. Breadth 0.58 metres.
Height 0.63 metres.

Note: This coffin is not illustrated.

THUTMOSE I.　　　18th Dynasty.　　　1524-1518 B.C.

The son of Amenhotep I and Queen Senseneb (a non-royal wife of the King) Thutmose married his half sister Princess Ahmose, to secure the throne.

Original tomb in the Valley of the Kings, Number 38.

The Mummy: Found in the Royal Cache at Deir el Bahri in 1881.
Cairo Museum Catalogue Number **61065.**
Exhibition Number **6345.**

Elliot Smith states that this mummy is "supposed to be that of Thutmose I". Maspero found that the coffins marked with the name of Thutmose I had been usurped by Pinudjem I. The mummy contained in these coffins was identified as that of Thutmose I after it had been unwrapped, as it bore a "striking resemblance" to the mummies of Thutmose II and Thutmose III. The mummy of Pinudjem I has not been found (or identified).

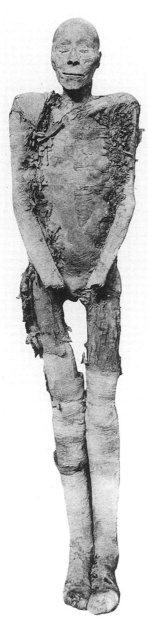

The mummy of Thutmose I (Fig 43)

From the variations in the mummification methods used, Elliot Smith dated this mummy after Ahmose, but before Thutmose II. The body is no longer covered by a layer of bituminous paste as were the earlier mummies and it is remarkable for the state of preservation, with a firm and durable skin.

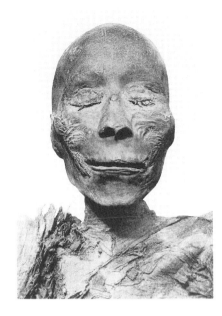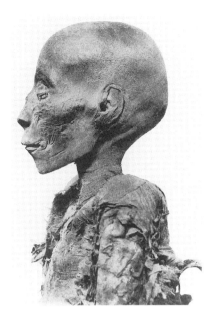

The head of the mummy of Thutmose I (Figs 44 and 45)

The arms were originally positioned with the hands (now missing) in the genital area, whereas from the time of Thutmose II onwards, the arms are crossed over the chest. Elliot Smith, therefore, confirmed Maspero's identification. Thutmose I was only 1.545 metres tall and it was pointed out that the other kings of this name were also of supposedly short stature.

Elliot Smith estimated the age of the King at death to be around fifty, which fits in well with the known length of his reign.

X-Rays showed that like other Pharaohs, Thutmose I suffered from rheumatoid arthritis and that at some time in his life he fractured his pelvis. They also showed that the King was physically different from Amenhotep. This casts serious doubts about the correct identification of this mummy, especially as experts who have studied the X-Rays are convinced that they are of the body of a young man, aged between eighteen and twenty. This is one of the problems which will only be resolved by future research.

The Coffins: Cairo Museum Catalogue Numbers 61024 and 61025.
Exhibition Number 3889.

Two coffins were used for the re-burial of Thutmose I. One was probably one of the original coffins used for the burial of the King.

The first coffin (no. 61024) has been dated to the 18th Dynasty and was probably made for Thutmose I and re-modelled for Pinudjem I.

The second coffin (no. 61025) is of the 21st Dynasty, having been brought into service for the re-burial of the King.

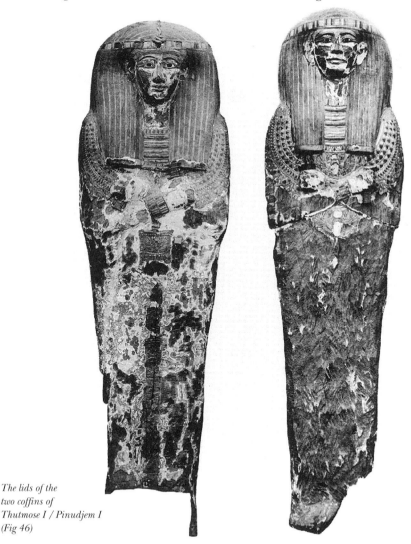

The lids of the two coffins of Thutmose I / Pinudjem I (Fig 46)

These coffins were re-used for the burial in the 21st Dynasty, of Pinudjem I.

It is possible that the mummy of Thutmose I had been moved several times, following the plundering of his tomb. If the mummy had been moved with others it may have been separated from the coffins in a subsequent robbery. The Priests would appear to have re-united the body of Thutmose I with its original coffin (assuming the identification is correct). Both coffins are made from cedar wood. A layer of white plaster covers the wood; this was originally overlaid with a thin layer of gold. Little, if any, of this gold remains on the coffins today; it has been hacked away, probably by members of the Abd er Rassul family, in the last century. Whatever tools they used for the task have left their marks on the bodies and faces of the coffins.

When complete, the decoration of both coffins would have been similar, although the facial characteristics of each coffin are quite different.

Crossed hands on the coffins hold the symbols of the God Osiris and the Goddess Isis.

Length of the outer coffin, 2.32 metres. Breadth 0.72 metres. Height 0.61 metres.

Length of the inner coffin, 2.12 metres. Breadth 0.60 metres. Height 0.21 metres.

THUTMOSE II.   18th Dynasty.   1518-1504 B.C.

Son of Thutmose I, Thutmose II married his half-sister Hatshepsut and ruled jointly with her. A non-royal wife, Isis, gave Thutmose a son, who was to rule after him.

Original tomb unknown.

The Mummy: Found in the Royal Cache at Deir el Bahri in 1881.
Cairo Museum Catalogue Number 61066.
Exhibition Number 6346.

The mummy of Thutmose II was unwrapped by Maspero on July 1st 1886. The body had been badly damaged by the robbers, in their search for valuables, but Elliot Smith was able to piece the body back together again.

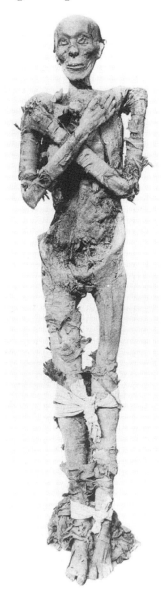

The mummy of Thutmose II (Fig 47)

The whole of the anterior abdominal wall and part of the thoracic wall had been hacked through by a large, heavy and sharp implement, probably an axe. The right leg was completely broken away from the body, also as the result of an axe cut.

There are cuts on the neck and two small cuts are visible on the chin.

The arms had been broken, but from the folds which remained in the skin, it was evident that they had once been crossed over the chest.

The skin of the thorax, shoulders and arms is covered with raised scabrous patches. Elliot Smith was not sure if these were a result of the embalming process and, therefore, post-mortem, or the evidence of some disease. It is interesting to note that similar patches appear on the bodies of Thutmose III and Amenhotep II, the immediate successors of Thutmose II. Modern scientific examination might be able to shed some light on this.

Unlike many of the Royal mummies, the finger nails and toe nails of Thutmose II were all neatly trimmed and clean.

Maspero gave Thutmose an age at death of thirty and based his estimate upon the state of the upper teeth, which are visible through the partly open mouth of the mummy. The X-Rays confirmed this age and have also shown that there is a close similarity between the bodies of Thutmose II and Thutmose I, so much so, that the Michigan team stated that the two bodies appeared almost like twin brothers, rather than father and son.

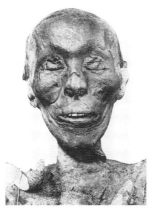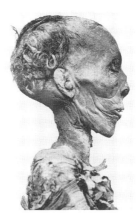

The head of the mummy
of Thutmose II
(Figs 48 and 49)

The head of the mummy is well preserved; the King, although balding, has a reasonable head of hair, whilst his predecessor had a shaven head.

Despite the packing of the nostrils by the embalmers, the fleshy part of the nose has been flattened by the pressure of the bandages. The packing can clearly be seen, as can the plugs blocking the ears.

Length of the body 1.684 metres.

The Coffin: Cairo Museum Catalogue Number **61013**.
Exhibition Number 3890.

The mummy of Thutmose II was found in a coffin remarkably similar to that of Amenhotep I. Both were probably made about the same time, during the 18th Dynasty.

Once again originally non-royal, this coffin has been adapted for Royal use. The identity of the original owner is not known.

A heavy black wig frames the face of the coffin; a Royal Uraeus would appear to have been added to the brow, but this has now been lost.

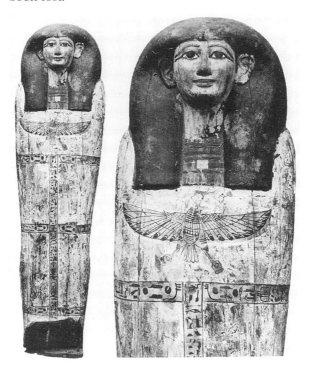

The lid of the coffin of Thutmose II (Fig 50)

Like the coffin of Amenhotep I, the titles of the King are written in black paint on yellow bands, which run down the centre and around the coffin. A vulture with wings outstretched, is crudely drawn on the chest of the coffin.

The coffin is made from cedar wood, which has been lightly plastered before painting.

Length of the coffin 1.95 metres. Breadth 0.55 metres.
Height 0.62 metres.

THUTMOSE III.   18th Dynasty.   1504-1450 B.C.

Son of Thutmose II, Thutmose III succeeded his father when aged only nine, but Queen Hatshepsut took the throne. Thutmose later co-reigned with Hatshepsut and became sole King on her death.

Thutmose III was one of the greatest of the warrior Pharaohs and during his reign the frontiers of Egypt were greatly extended. Tribute began to flow into Egypt and the temples of the great God Amun, at Thebes, benefited greatly from this influx of wealth. Original tomb in the Valley of the Kings, Number 34.

The Mummy: Found in the Royal Cache at Deir el Bahri in 1881.
Cairo Museum Catalogue Number **61068**.
Exhibition Number **6347**.

The mummy of Thutmose III was the first of the Royal mummies to be unwrapped in July 1881. It was then re-wrapped and subsequently unwrapped again in 1886.

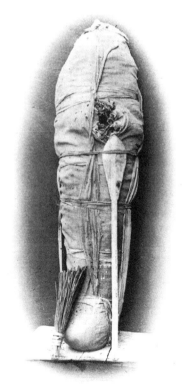

The wrapped mummy of Thutmose III (Fig 51)

Even before the unwrapping, it was obvious that this mummy was in a poor state, for the priests who had arranged the re-burial had used wooden oar-shaped pieces of wood as splints, to strengthen the body. Four such splints were used, placed on the outside of the body and within the bandages. (These splints were probably part of the funerary equipment of a Royal burial for similar oars were found in the burial chamber of the tomb of Tutankhamun).

Modern robbers had also damaged further the wrapped mummy, for a hole had been made in the bandages, at the level of the heart, in an attempt to locate any remaining jewellery on the body.

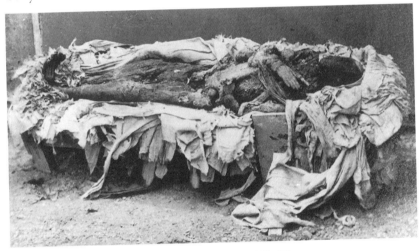

The mummy of Thutmose III (Fig 52)

The unwrapping was a rapid affair; a photograph of the event shows the body lying in a veritable 'explosion' of bandages, which had simply been cut through to reach the body as quickly as possible. The few mummy unwrappings which have taken place in recent years have taken far longer, with each layer of the bandages being removed a layer at a time and each subject to a detailed examination.

The body of Thutmose III when revealed had been badly treated by the ancient tomb robbers. All the limbs had been detached from the body. The arms were crossed over the chest and the left hand was in a flexed position, which suggests that it may originally have held a cylindrical object about 2.3 centimetres in diameter, such as one of the Royal emblems, the Crook or the Flail.

Maspero and Brugsch were both greatly discouraged by the state of this mummy and immediate plans to unwrap further mummies were abandoned for they thought that all the others would also be badly damaged.

X-Rays show that the body was of a similar build to both Thutmose I and Thutmose II.

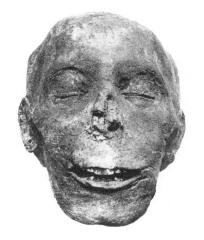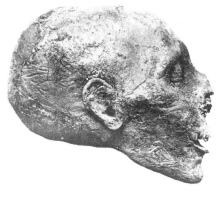

The head of the mummy of Thutmose III
(Figs 53 and 54)

The teeth are worn, but show none of the more severe dental problems experienced by later Pharaohs.

A few items of jewellery remained on the body, despite the attempts of the tomb robbers. A wide bracelet and a twist of wire was found on the right arm, although these were probably added by the priests who restored the burial. A few beads of carnelian, gold and lapis lazuli were also found in two strings within the wrappings in the area of the shoulders.

Thutmose ruled Egypt for fifty-five years and must, therefore, have been well into his sixties when he died, although the X-Rays do not lend support to such an advanced age.

The head, although detached from the body, is well preserved, apart from the nose which has been both flattened and broken.

Like Thutmose I, the head of Thutmose III has been shaved. Clearly there was no ritual requirement for the hair to be removed as some Pharaohs have full heads of hair. The presence of hair or otherwise must have been the personal preference of each King.

Elliot Smith recorded the length of the mummy at 1.615 metres.

Thutmose III is often described as 'The Napoleon of Ancient Egypt', both for his military exploits and for his supposedly short stature. In the *Journal of Human Evolution*, number 12, 1983, Robins and Shute point out that Elliot Smith had omitted the fact that the feet of Thutmose III were missing, not surprising considering the damaged state of the mummy. The living stature of Thutmose III has been estimated by Robins and Shute from the length of the long bones of the body which were compared to other bodies. This results in a height for Thutmose III of 1.71 metres. Thutmose was, it would appear, far from being undersized and his height compares well with other Royal mummies from this period.

The Coffin: Cairo Museum Catalogue Number **61014**.
            Exhibition Number **3887**.

The coffin of Thutmose III has suffered almost as much as his mummy, at the hands of tomb-robbers, both ancient and modern. It is, however, probably one of his original coffins, which shows the King wearing the Nemes head-dress.

Made of cedar wood, what we see today is the 'inner core' of what was probably a particularly fine coffin. The wood was covered with a layer of linen and plaster which was overlaid by a layer of thin gold, little of which now remains. The outer two coffins of Tutankhamun probably have a wooden core similar to this.

A mask of thicker gold would have covered the face, and probably the hands, which are crossed over the chest and would have held the Royal insignia.

The inlaid eyes of the coffin have been lost. Decoration on the body of the coffin would probably have been of the 'rishi' type, as seen on both earlier and later coffins.

The interior of the coffin was also gilded, and the titles and names of the King survive on the inside of the lid.

Length of the coffin 2.07 metres. Breadth 0.67 metres.
Height 0.63 metres.

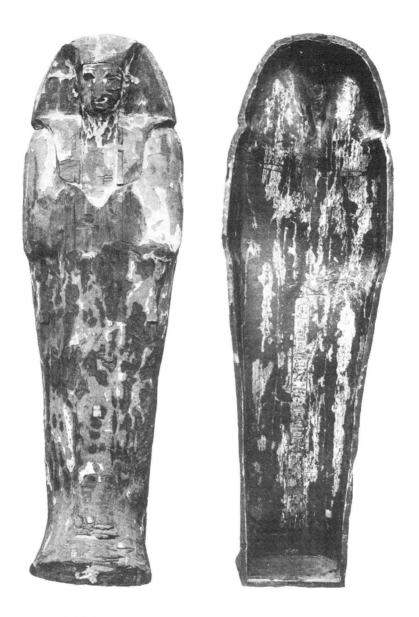

The lid of the coffin of Thutmose III: Exterior and Interior views (Fig 55)

AMENHOTEP II.   18th Dynasty.   1453-1419 B.C.

Son of Thutmose III, Amenhotep ruled jointly with his father for a few years before succeeding to the throne. His mother was Meritre, daughter of Queen Hatshepsut. Amenhotep followed the warrior traditions of his father and was renowned for his athletic abilities. Original tomb in the Valley of the Kings, Number 35.

The Mummy: Found in his own tomb in the Valley of the Kings at Luxor in 1898. Cairo Museum Exhibition Number 6348.

The burial of Amenhotep had also been disturbed anciently by tomb robbers. The priests of the 21st Dynasty restored his burial in his own tomb, the location of which must have appeared secure, for other royal burials were moved into the tomb in the Valley of the Kings.

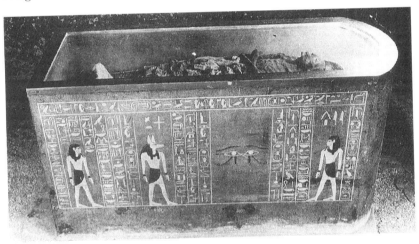

The mummy of Amenhotep II displayed in his sarcophagus in his tomb in the Valley of the Kings (Fig 56)

After the tomb was re-discovered the body of the King was left on display, still enclosed in the pink granite sarcophagus. It was not until 'modern' tomb-robbers once again entered the tomb in a vain hope that something of value might remain on the body and have been overlooked by the archaeologists, that it was moved to join the main collection of Royal mummies in Cairo.

Amenhotep has a marked resemblance to both his father, Thutmose III and his son, Thutmose IV. He was taller than most of Egypt's rulers and was an able athlete, often boasting on his monuments of his talents as a soldier and hunter. The body was badly damaged by the repeated robberies.

Elliot Smith estimated the age of the King at death to between forty and fifty. X-Rays confirmed the age at around forty-five and also showed that the King probably suffered in later life from rheumatoid arthritis.

The head is covered with wavy brown hair which has turned grey at the temples. There is a small bald spot at the crown of his head.

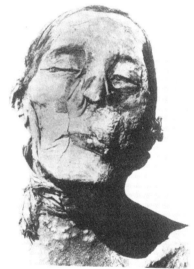

The head of the mummy of Amenhotep II (Fig 57)

The skin of the neck, shoulders, thorax and abdomen is covered in small nodules. Their cause is not yet known and will probably only be established at a full scientific investigation.

Height of the body 1.673 metres.

The Coffin:

It has not been possible to find a photograph or description of the coffin which contained the body of Amenhotep II. When the two volumes of the 'Catalogue' were produced for the Cairo Museum, the mummy (and possibly the coffin) remained in the tomb. In the volume on the mummies, no photographic plate of the mummy was included, although there was a description of the body.

The tomb of Amenhotep II was amongst the first in the Valley of the Kings to be lit by electricity and a light was placed directly over the face of the mummy. The tomb guides would extinguish all the lights in the tomb apart from this one, leaving the features of the King revealed against the darkness.

UNKNOWN WOMAN.   18th Dynasty.   Date uncertain.

The Mummy: Found in the Tomb of Amenhotep II in 1898.
            Cairo Museum Catalogue Number **61072.**

This uncoffined mummy was discovered in a side chamber in the tomb of Amenhotep II along with the mummies of a Prince and a second female mummy, now identified as Queen Tiye.

Because of the close-shaven head, this mummy was originally believed to be that of a young man. Elliot Smith determined it was the body of a young woman from the anatomical evidence.

Badly damaged by robbers, the exterior wall of the chest has been smashed and the left side of the mouth broken away. The right arm has been torn off below the shoulder.

Nothing survives to identify this woman, who may have been one of the original occupants of the tomb, perhaps belonging to the family of Amenhotep II.

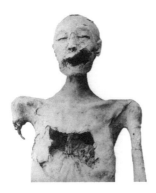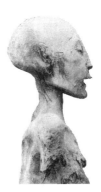

The mummy of an Unknown Woman (Figs 58 and 59)

The association of this mummy with Queen Tiye and the Prince (possibly Crown Prince Thutmose, son of Amenhotep III and Queen Tiye) has led to the belief that the correct identity may be

Queen/Princess Sitamun. Sitamun was the daughter of Amenhotep III and Queen Tiye and may have been the mother of Tutankhamun and Smenkhkare.

The mummy still remains in the re-sealed side chamber of the tomb.

Length of the body 1.580 metres.

THE MUMMY OF A PRINCE.   18th Dynasty. c.1440 B.C.

The Mummy: Found in the tomb of Amenhotep II in 1898.
Cairo Museum Catalogue Number **61071**.

This mummy was found in a side chamber of the tomb of Amenhotep II, along with two female mummies, one now identified as that of Queen Tiye, the other still unidentified.

Nothing is known of this Prince. Elliot Smith dated the mummy to the 18th Dynasty by the method of embalming. The fact that it was found in the tomb of Amenhotep II, may indicate that he was a son of this King. During this period the burials of the Queens and Princes were often made in the tomb of the King.

Elliot Smith in his Catalogue identified this mummy as "probably the Royal Prince Ouabkhousenou", but this identification is suspect as it is based on the discovery of some wooden funerary figures, found elsewhere in the tomb of Amenhotep II, which bore the names of both Amenhotep and Ouabkhousenou. The association of this mummy with Queen Tiye, has led to the belief that it may be that of Prince Thutmose, eldest son of Amenhotep III and Queen Tiye.

Bodies of Princes are relatively rare finds, which is surprising, bearing in mind the probable high infant mortality rate at this time.

The prince was nine or ten years old at death, certainly no more than eleven. His head is shaved, apart from the traditional 'side lock of youth' often seen in reliefs and sculptures. This sign of youth would have been removed when the Prince reached maturity. The hair is some 27.5 centimetres long and it would appear that it was once plaited.

The ears have been pierced according to the fashion of the time.

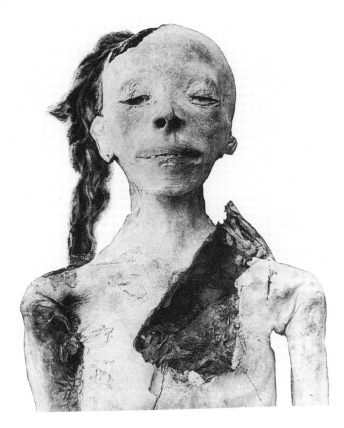

The mummy of a Prince (Fig 60)

This mummy was not enclosed in any coffin and has been badly damaged by the tomb robbers.

It still remains sealed in the side chamber in the tomb of Amenhotep II.

Height of the body 1.242 metres.

UNKNOWN WOMAN.   18th Dynasty.   Date Uncertain.

This small tomb in the Valley of the Kings was discovered by Howard Carter in 1903, whilst he was excavating at the entrance to tomb KV 19 (owned by Prince Montuherkopeshef of the 20th Dynasty).

The Tomb:

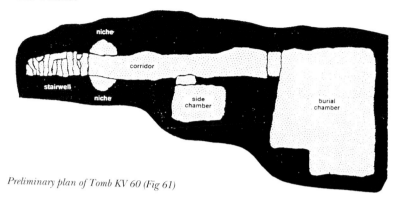

Preliminary plan of Tomb KV 60 (Fig 61)

Only fragments of the original burial remained in the undecorated burial chamber. Carter gave the discovery only a brief mention in his publications. The contents included two female mummies, one in an inscribed coffin, and some mummified geese. Uninterested in the find, Carter re-sealed the tomb, leaving the contents intact.

In 1906 Edward Ayrton re-opened the tomb (now numbered KV 60) whilst he was clearing tomb KV 19. It must have been then that the coffined mummy was moved to the Cairo Museum. This coffin is inscribed with the name of Sitre, who was nurse to Queen Hatshepsut.

Ayrton re-sealed the tomb and the exact location of the site was soon lost. American Egyptologist Donald Ryan re-discovered this lost tomb in 1989 and has re-excavated it, finding the debris-strewn tomb of more interest to a modern archaeologist than to Howard Carter.

The results of this new excavation have not yet been published.

The Mummy: Found in Tomb KV60 in the Valley of the Kings in 1903 (re-located in 1989).

This uncoffined mummy was found lying in the centre of the undecorated burial chamber of the tomb.

The mummy was mostly unwrapped and on its back. Strands of reddish-blond hair lay on the floor beneath the bald head.

The left arm is bent at the elbow to bring a loosely clenched fist over the centre of the chest. The right arm lies along the right side of the body with the fingers unflexed. This appears to be an 18th Dynasty position for a female Royal mummy. The pose is identical to that of the 'Elder Lady' found in the tomb of Amenhotep II and now identified as that of Queen Tiye. There are, however, too few surviving 18th Dynasty female Royal mummies to be certain that this particular position was always adopted.

The nails of the clenched hand are painted red and outlined in black.

An initial study of the mummy in 1989 concluded that she had been quite fat in life, because of the large folds of dried skin noted on her buttocks.

The teeth appear to be well worn, which suggests an older individual.

The embalming incision is, unusually, through the pelvic floor, rather than on the side of the abdomen, which may well be because of the obesity of the lady at her death. Apart from this, the embalming techniques used and the appearance of the mummy indicate an 18th Dynasty date.

Elizabeth Thomas, author of *The Royal Necropoleis of Thebes*, tentatively and speculatively suggested that this mummy could be that of Queen Hatshepsut, whose original tomb lies close by. When tomb KV60 was first discovered it also contained the mummy of the nurse of Queen Hatshepsut. As the tomb at this time was 'lost', Thomas' idea that this might be Hatshepsut was based on the brief notes on the tomb and the mummy, written by Howard Carter.

Donald Ryan, who re-discovered the tomb, has pointed out that any positive identification of this mummy is not possible at this stage and that the speculative identification is based on circumstantial evidence.

A fragment of coffin face survives, badly damaged and covered in adze marks, which indicate that it was probably once covered in gold. There is a notch at the chin which may once have held a beard.

Hatshepsut assumed the role of King and was portrayed as such on her monuments. She may have been buried in a 'male' coffin (although it could be argued that in this case the body would be expected to have been placed in the usual male position). Little inscribed material remains in the tomb which might help any identification of the mummy and the fragments found are inconclusive.

A full scientific examination of the mummy, including the use of X-Rays, has yet to be made.

Height of the body 1.55 metres.

The mummy has been placed in a simple modern wooden coffin and, at the moment, remains in the tomb.

Note: A photograph of this mummy is not available.

QUEEN MERYET-AMUN   18th Dynasty.   c.1440 B.C.

Little is known about the life of Meryet-Amun. She was probably the eldest daughter of Thutmose III and wife of Amenhotep II. She must have died soon after her coronation, for it was Queen Tio who was to become the principal wife of Amenhotep II and the mother of the next Pharaoh.

Her mummy was found in her tomb at Deir el Bahri, located immediately adjacent to the temple of Queen Hatshepsut. The tomb was re-discovered in 1929 by H. E. Winlock, leader of an excavation organised by the Metropolitan Museum of Art. Like virtually all the other Royal burials, this one too had been robbed in antiquity and the burial restored by the priests of the 21st Dynasty.

The Tomb:

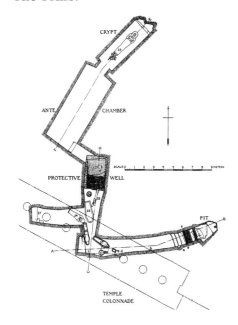

Plan of the the tomb of Queen Meryet-Amun (Fig 62)

Now numbered DB 358, this tomb was discovered on February 23rd 1929.

The tomb entrance corridor is situated virtually directly under the northern colonnade of the first terrace of the funerary temple of Queen Hatshepsut at Deir el Bahri. It must have been cut after the foundations of the temple were laid, for some of the blocks intrude into the roof of the corridor. Had the foundations been cut from the rock after the construction of the corridor, the void would have undoubtedly caused the roof to collapse.

Like so many other Royal tombs, it had received the attentions of robbers and had been ransacked. The priests of the 21st Dynasty restored the burial and re-sealed the tomb.

The tomb was also used for a later Royal burial, that of Princess Entiu-ny, a daughter of Pinudjem I of the 21st Dynasty. As she was at least seventy years old when she died, her burial must have taken place in the reign of one of the successors of Pinudjem and, therefore, well after the restoration of the burial.

From the disorganised state of this later burial, it is clear that the tomb may have been re-discovered by accident. The workers were unprepared for the protective well cut in the tomb. This effectively blocked their progress and meant that the body of Entiu-ny could not be placed in the burial chamber, where the huge coffin and mummy of Queen Meryet-Amun remained undisturbed.

It is also evident that the workmen used their time in the tomb effectively and removed the gilt faces and hands from Entiu-ny's coffins. They did not even bother to close the two coffins properly. The bodies and lids were scattered around the first corridors of the Tomb.

The Mummy: Found in her own tomb at Deir el Bahri in 1929.
Cairo Museum Catalogue Number 55150.
Exhibition Number 6362.

Winlock arranged for the unwrapping of the mummy. Most of the 18th Dynasty wrappings had been removed by the robbers, who had taken the valuable items of jewellery from the body. Only impressions made by the objects on the skin of the body remained, although enough evidence was retrieved this way to enable reconstructions of some of the pieces to be made. Fragments of a girdle remained on the body.

At the time of her death, Meryet-Amun was about fifty years old. She was short with a delicately formed figure. Her face is wide across

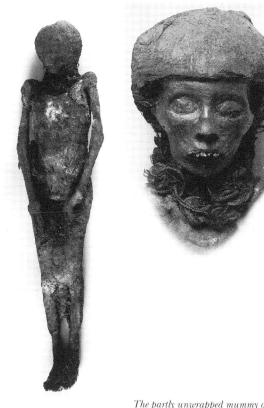

The partly unwrapped mummy of Queen Meryet-Amun (Fig 63)

the cheeks, with a high bridged nose and a slender pointed chin.

Her hair is brown, with no traces of grey and is wavy. As seen in other mummies, the natural hair is interwoven with fake braids and tresses of hair the same colour as her own.

The body had been covered with liquid resin with a thicker layer of resin paste covering the face. Her features and relatively large head, bear a strong resemblance to her father, Thutmose III.

Height of the body 1.545 metres.

The Coffins: The First Coffin; Cairo Museum Catalogue Number 53141.

The first coffin of the Queen is skilfully made of cedar wood. The appearance of this coffin today owes much to the 21st Dynasty restorers.

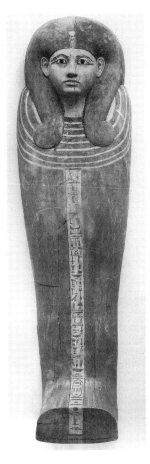

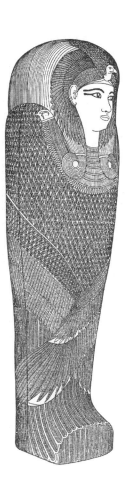

The coffin was originally covered in sheet gold on a plaster base. It would have been incised with the familiar 'rishi' feather design.

Robbers must have stripped all the gold from the coffin, revealing the wooden core, which was painted by the restorers. The hair was painted blue and a yellow Uraeus added to the brow to replace the lost vulture head. The damaged eyebrows were restored in blue glass paste; the original alabaster and obsidian eyes remained. A collar was painted in alternate strips of yellow and blue and the body of the coffin painted red.

Down the front of the coffin a painted inscription was added, blue on a yellow ground, giving the names and titles of the Queen. This was copied sign for sign from the inscription on the second coffin.

Length of the coffin 1.85 metres.

The second coffin: Catalogue Number 53140.
Exhibition Number 6150.

The second coffin has truly gigantic measurements. It is especially large when compared to the first coffin.

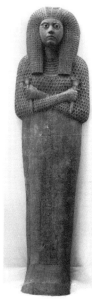

The lid of the second coffin of Queen Meryet-Amun (Fig 67)

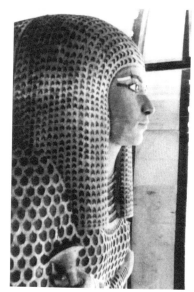

The Metropolitan Museum of Art Egyptian Expedition 1929-1930

The second coffin of Queen Meryet-Amun (Fig 68)

This coffin too is made with great skill of fine cedar. It is similar in design to other Queens' coffins which survive from the same period.

The appearance of this coffin has also changed. The face and hands were probably left in the natural wood. Original eyes survive although the eyebrows have been restored.

The wig is covered with sunken chevrons representing braided hair and the arms and breast of the coffin with scales representing feathers.

The sunken areas contain remains of plaster which shows the impressions of lost inlays, which would have been of coloured glass paste. The raised areas have traces of a linen backing for plaster, which shows that these parts of the coffin would have originally been gilded. The restorers painted the areas which were once gold yellow and the inlaid areas a green/blue.

The papyrus umbels held in the hands were probably gilded. The lower part of the coffin would also have been covered with gold, and decorated in the usual 'rishi' feather design.

There was originally a third coffin which enclosed the first two.

Only shattered fragments of this coffin remain, which was made of a coarser wood, probably tamarisk. It would have been at least 3.25 metres in length and similar in design to the first coffin. Fragments also survived of a wooden sarcophagus. Both this and the third coffin must have been so badly damaged by the tomb robbers that restoration by the 21st Dynasty priests was not possible.

Length of the coffin 3.135 metres. Breadth 0.87 metres.

THUTMOSE IV.   18th Dynasty.   1419-1386 B.C.

Son of Amenhotep II and Queen Tio, Thutmose IV is best known to us today because of the stela he erected between the paws of the great Sphinx at Giza. Whilst still a prince he dreamed that the Sphinx promised he would become King if he cleared the sand from it. The sand was cleared and Thutmose became King. Original tomb in the Valley of the Kings, number 43, discovered by Howard Carter in 1902.

The Mummy: Found in the tomb of Amenhotep II in 1898.
            Cairo Museum Catalogue Number 61073.
            Exhibition Number 6349.

The mummy of Thutmose IV was unwrapped by Daressy in Cairo on 26th March 1903. The unwrapping revealed the body of an extremely emaciated man, slightly bald, who died at the age of thirty or less.

Both arms are crossed over the chest and the flexed hands once held cylindrical objects 1.5 centimetres in diameter (probably the Crook and the Flail, symbols of sovereignty). The finger nails are well manicured, which show that the King was well cared for before his death, although the crude embalming incision suggests a hasty and unprofessional job.

The Michigan team were of the opinion that the emaciated condition of the body was not just the result of the embalming, but of a disease which may well have contributed to the King's death. Only future tissue-sampling will verify this.

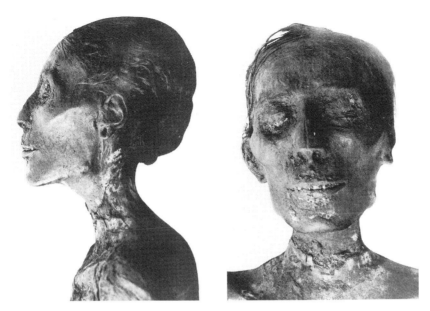

The head of the mummy of Thutmose IV (Figs 69 and 70)

The mummy bears a close resemblance to Amenhotep II, which helps to confirm the known order of succession.

Height of the body 1.646 metres.

The Coffin: Cairo Museum Catalogue Number **61035**.
                      Exhibition Number **3882**.

Thutmose IV was buried in a 20th Dynasty coffin made of sycamore.

The expected Royal insignia are missing from the coffin, which was probably originally made for a non-royal burial.

The coffin is painted white, apart from the face which is coloured red.

A single band of hieroglyphs runs down the front of the coffin, giving the names and titles of the King.

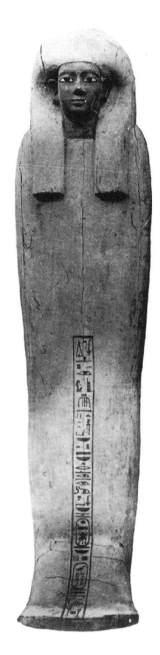

The lid of the coffin of Thutmose IV (Fig 71)

Length of the coffin 1.89 metres. Breadth 0.49 metres.
Height 0.63 metres.

MAIHERPRI 18th Dynasty Date Uncertain.

The name Maiherpri means 'The Lion on the Battlefields' and from this it is evident that Maiherpri was a warrior. This is confirmed by the large number of military items discovered in his tomb. One of his official titles was 'Fan Bearer on the King's Right Hand' and he was either a relative or a close companion of a King. The fact that his tomb was built in the Royal Valley confirms this.

Evidence to connect Maiherpri with any particular King is lacking. Various Kings have been suggested including Amenhotep II and Amenhotep III. Thutmose IV is probably the most likely candidate.

The Tomb: KV 36.

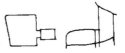

Plan and side view of the tomb of Maiherpri (Fig 72)

The tomb of Maiherpri was discovered by Loret in March 1899. The burial was relatively intact which made it at the time one of the more important tombs discovered in the Valley.

The details of the excavation of the tomb were not well recorded and a full account has never been published.

The burial had been disturbed by robbers and none of the contents lay in their original positions. The robbers had taken all the portable metal objects and items of linen and clothing.

Curiously enough, jars containing oil remained untouched. We know that oil was a valuable commodity and it is possible that the oil had become rancid by the time the tomb was plundered, which suggests that the tomb may not have been robbed until some years after the burial. It is possible that this tomb was located by accident when other tombs were being dug in the vicinity. At some point the robbery was discovered and the tomb was hastily covered up and re-sealed.

Included in the objects discovered in the tomb was a fine papyrus, illustrating the Book of the Dead. Maiherpri is shown offering to the Gods and whilst he is shown with the normal profile of men of the period, his skin is painted dark brown rather than the usual red ochre and his hair is shown as being short and curly. At various times in recent history, the racial origins of the Ancient Egyptians have excited a great deal of interest and this papyrus clearly shows how different skin colours were accurately depicted and that a darker skin was the exception rather than the rule.

The Mummy: Cairo Museum Catalogue Number **24100.**

The mummy of Maiherpri was unwrapped on the 22nd March 1901, two years after the discovery of the tomb. Various small items of jewellery, which had been missed by the robbers, were found on the mummy.

The well preserved body of Maiherpri was revealed, showing him to be negroid, possibly of Nubian origin.

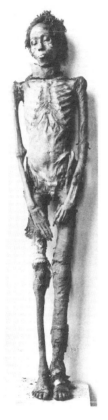

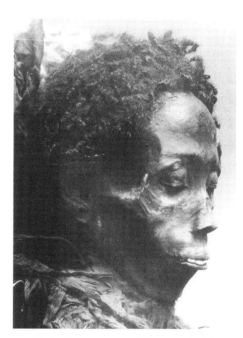

The head of the mummy of Maiherpri (Fig 74)

The mummy of Maiherpri (Fig 73)

The black curly hair is actually a wig and the ears are pierced. Maiherpri was probably only about twenty when he died. The cause of his death is unknown and there are no indications evident on the mummy.

Height of the body 1.64 metres.

The Coffins:

The mummy was found contained in three coffins. A fourth coffin lay empty in the tomb. Maspero thought that it might have been used to convey the body to the tomb, but this is unlikely. It is more probable that this coffin was intended to be enclosed within the other coffins, but that it was made the wrong size and would not fit within the other coffins as intended.

The First Coffin: Cairo Museum Catalogue Number 24001.

This rectangular coffin is made of planks of cedar. The sides and ends were each made separately and later assembled, possibly in the tomb. Carpenter's marks on each corner helped to ensure the pieces were fitted correctly.

    The whole coffin, interior and exterior, is covered in thick black bitumen. Gilded plaster panels of inscriptions and figures of the gods decorate the coffin. The decoration of this coffin is similar to the outer coffins of Yuya and Thuya, which are only slightly later in date.

Length of the coffin 2.81 metres. Breadth 1.02 metres. Height (including the lid) 1.38 metres.

The Second Coffin: Cairo Museum Catalogue Number 24002.

    This anthropoid coffin was contained in the rectangular outer coffin. The face, parts of the head-dress, the collar and the hands are gilded. The coffin has fine inlaid eyes and a carved wooden beard adorns the chin.

Length of the coffin 2.55 metres. Breadth 0.80 metres.
Height 0.96 metres.

NOTE: This coffin is not illustrated.

The Third Coffin: Cairo Museum Catalogue Number **24003.**

This coffin was not used to contain the mummy and when the tomb was discovered, lay overturned beside the outer coffin. It was probably intended to be the innermost of the set of three anthropoid coffins.

Made of cedar, this coffin too has gilding on the face, head-dress, collar, hands and on bands of inscriptions and figures of the Gods which decorate the coffin.

This coffin has fine inlaid eyes, but no beard.

Length of the coffin 2.18 metres. Breadth 0.65 metres.
Height 0.87 metres.

The Fourth Coffin: Cairo Museum Catalogue Number **24004.**

This exceptionally well preserved coffin contained the mummy of Maiherpri and is again anthropoid in shape and is decorated in a similar way to the other coffins. The face of the coffin is finely carved, with inlaid eyes and a beard adorns the chin.

No dimensions are given in the Cairo Museum Catalogue for this coffin.

The Mask: Cairo Museum Catalogue Number **24096.**

The head and upper part of the mummy were covered in a fine and well preserved funerary mask made of cartonnage. The interior is coated with bitumen and the exterior is painted black with the face gold and gold bands on both the head-dress and collar.

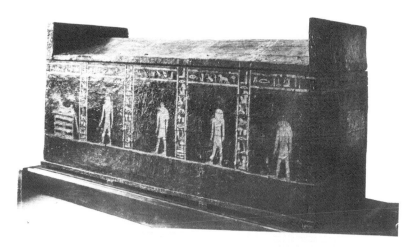

The first coffin of Maiherpri (Fig 75)

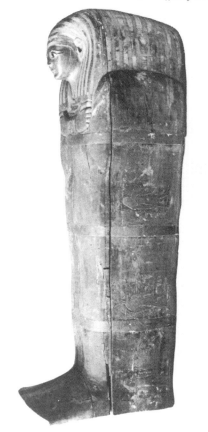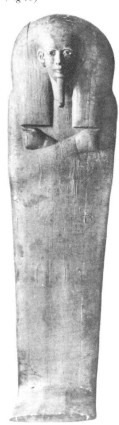

The third and fourth coffins of Maiherpri (Fig 76)

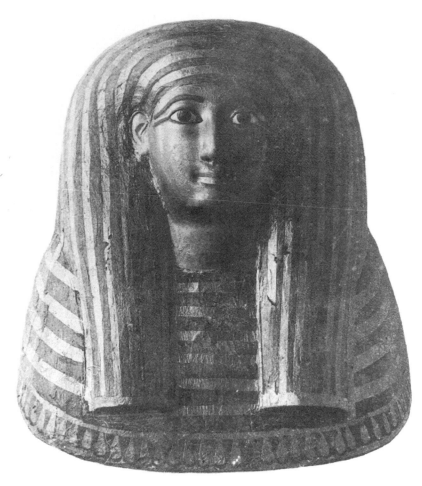

The mask of Maiherpri (Fig 77)

Yuya and Thuya.   18th Dynasty.   1403-1365 B.C.

The tomb of Yuya and Thuya was discovered in the Valley of the Kings in 1905.

Yuya and Thuya were the parents of Queen Tiye, Great Wife of King Amenhotep III.

Yuya was originally a priest and his wife was a Mistress of the Robes in the temple of the God Min at Akhmim, from where they both originated.

With the marriage of their daughter, favours were given to them by the King and Yuya was appointed Commander of the Chariots. (A chariot was actually included in his funeral equipment).

The couple were given the honour of being allowed a tomb in the Valley of the Kings, a rare privilege for commoners.

Although robbed in antiquity, the tomb yielded many spectacular objects. The coffins are some of the finest ever found and the mummies are amongst the best preserved.

It is clear from the different methods of embalming used that Yuya and Thuya died at different times and that the tomb was re-opened to accommodate the second burial.

The tomb: KV46

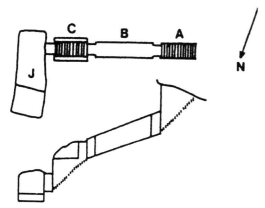

Plan and elevation of the tomb of Yuya and Thuya. (Fig 78)

The tomb of Yuya and Thuya, the parents of Queen Tiye, was discovered by Theodore Davis on February 5th 1905. The entrance to the tomb in the Valley of the Kings (now numbered KV 46) had been completely concealed by chippings produced during the building of the tombs of Ramesses III (KV 3) and Ramesses XI (KV 4). Tomb KV 3 was unused by Ramesses III, who constructed a much larger tomb for himself in the Valley (KV 11).

The sealings of the tomb were still in place, but it was immediately evident that the tomb has been plundered in antiquity and re-sealed.

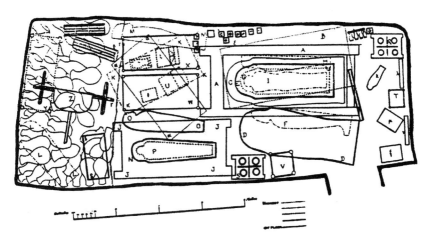

Plan of the Burial Chamber the tomb of Yuya and Thuya (Fig 79)

A. Canopy of Yuya, no 51001.
B. Its lid. no 51001.
C. Second coffin of Yuya, no 51002.
D. Its lid.
E. Third coffin of Yuya, no 51003.
F. Its lid.
G. Fourth coffin of Yuya, no 51004.
H. Its lid.
I. Mummy of Yuya, no 51190.
J. Outermost coffin of Thuya, no 51005.
K. Its lid.
L. Second (gilt) coffin of Thuya, no 51006.
M. Its lid.
N. Third coffin of Thuya, no 51007.
0. Its lid.
P. Mummy of Thuya, no 51196.
Q. Cartonnage cage, no 51011.
R. Canopic box of Yuya, no 51012.
S. Canopic box of Thuya, 51013.
T. Ibex chair, no 51111.

U. Gilt chair, no 51112.
V. Largest chair, no 51113.
W. Gilt bedstead, no 51110.
X. Painted bedstead, no 51108.
Y. Silvered bedstead, no 51109.
Z. Chariot, no 51188.
a. Side of coffin, no 51005.
b. Mat, no 51187.
c. Here the 18 boxes of provisions.
d. Wig-basket, no 51119.
e. Ushabtis in their shrines.
f. Jewel box of Yuya, no 51117.
g. Alabaster vase, no 51104.
h. Jewel-case of Thuya, no 51118.
i. Limestone vase on stand, no 51102.
j. Model coffin, no 51054.
k. Osiris bed.
l. Box, no 51115.
m. Osiris bed.
n. Box, no 51116.

Much of the funerary equipment remained, but mainly only the larger items, which included some splendid pieces of Royal furniture, chairs and chests, from the reign of Amenhotep III. At the time of the discovery, this was the richest find of modern times in the Valley of the Kings.

It is probable that the tomb was heavily robbed of all small portable and valuable items relatively soon after the burial was made.

The contents of this tomb are now on display in the Cairo Museum.

YUYA:

The Mummy: Cairo Museum Catalogue Number **51190**.

The robbers had badly damaged the linen bandages covering the mummy in their search for valuables. The outer layers were covered by a layer of black resin paste.

The body cavity is packed with linen soaked in resin which has now solidified. A gold plate still remains in place covering the embalming incision in the side of the body.

The body is that of an old man. The arms are flexed and folded across the chest with the hands meeting just under the chin.

The right hand is fully extended whilst the left is flexed. One gold finger stall remains on the little finger of the right hand. When the mummy was unwrapped, a set of these covered the end of each finger; their purpose was to hold the nails in position during the embalming process. The nails are very long.

Yuya had white hair, now stained yellow by the embalming. It is long (more than 11 centimetres) and wavy.

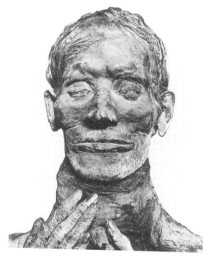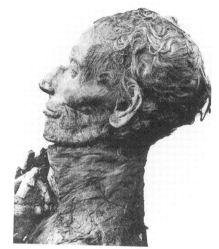

The head of the mummy of Yuya (Figs 80 and 81)

The beard and moustache had probably not been shaved for some two or three days before death. The eyebrows and eyelashes are well preserved.

Packing of linen in the nostrils has caused them to now appear dilated. The eye sockets are also packed with linen.

A thick coating of resin covers the genital area.

The internal organs were removed from the body and were placed in a Canopic Chest which was also found in the tomb.

The skin of the face is well preserved and wrinkled. The whole aspect of the face is of great dignity and repose and this is perhaps the best surviving mummy of the 18th Dynasty.

Yuya was probably in his sixties when he died.

X-Rays of the head show that the brain has been removed and the empty cavity filled with resin.

Height of the body 1.65 metres.

The Coffins:

The Sledge-Canopy: Cairo Museum Catalogue Number **51001**.
                       Exhibition Number **3668** .

A sledge-canopy formed the outermost of the set of coffins made for Yuya. It is in the form of a box on a sledge. The box has no bottom and the coffin it enclosed rested on the floor of the tomb.

Made of wood, the sledge canopy is covered in lustrous black pitch with raised gilt plaster decoration. Much of the gold is reddish in colour.

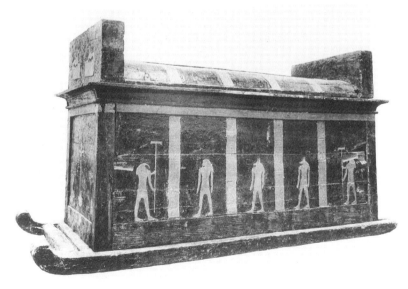

The sledge-canopy of Yuya (Fig 82)

The raised decorations in relief are made from a layer of plaster backed with cloth and glued to the body of the coffin. This decoration was applied before the background was painted black, as the gold is splashed in a number of places.

The wood planks have been carefully joined to make the required length. Any knots have been cut out and specially trimmed pieces of wood pegged into the holes.

The completed canopy was too large to be admitted to the tomb and was assembled and possibly painted in the burial chamber, which may account for the somewhat careless workmanship.

Total length, including the sledge 3.64 metres. Length of the coffin 3.22. metres. Breadth 1.605 metres. Height of the base 1.63 metres. Height of the lid 0.53 metres.

The Second Coffin: Cairo Museum Catalogue Number **51002.** Exhibition Number **3666.**

Made of wood, this huge second coffin is decorated in a similar way to the first, being covered with black pitch with raised details in gilt plaster.

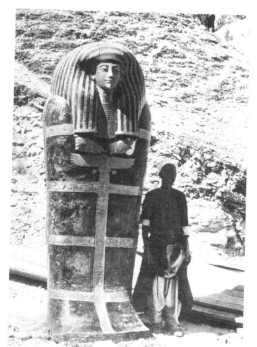

The second coffin of Yuya, standing outside the tomb, awaiting packing and transport to the Cairo Museum (Fig 83)

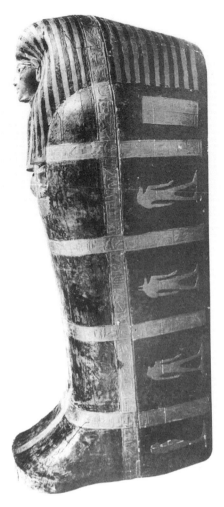

The second coffin of Yuya
(Fig 84)

A gilt band bearing an inscription runs down the centre of the lid, with other bands running around the body. The base of the coffin is decorated with gilt images of the Gods.

The wig is decorated with gilt stripes.

The eyes are inlaid with white calcite and black glass, with eyelids and eyebrows of blue glass.

The deceased is shown with his hands crossed over the chest.

Robbers have damaged the face and one hand of the lid when it was thrown to one side of the tomb.

The thin layer of plaster is cracked through in many places.

Length of the coffin 2.75 metres. Breadth 1.05 metres.
Height 1.26 metres.

The Third Coffin: Cairo Museum Catalogue Number **51003.**
Exhibition Number **3667.**

This coffin is covered with silver leaf with the inscriptions and figures of the Gods detailed in gold. Parts of the coloured glass inlay are missing.

The eyes are inlaid in the same manner as those of the second coffin.

The face is gilt with the wig decorated with alternate stripes of gold and silver.

A large inlaid necklace covers the top part of the coffin, fashioned out of pieces of coloured glass, light and dark blue and red. The inlay is set into the plaster and is separated by lines of gilt. Bracelets and the figure of a vulture are also inlaid.

Below the vulture, and extending down to the feet of the coffin, is a figure of the Goddess Nut, modelled in gilt plaster.

The inside of the coffin is covered in black pitch, with the figure of Nut painted in red on the lid and modelled in relief on the base.

The hands are crossed. One holds a symbol of the Goddess Isis, the other a symbol of the God Osiris. The silver decoration appears to have been applied to the coffin after the gold.

When first discovered the silver was still bright, but within two days it had blackened from exposure to the air.

Length of the coffin 2.27 metres. Breadth 0.77 metres.
Height 0.92 metres.

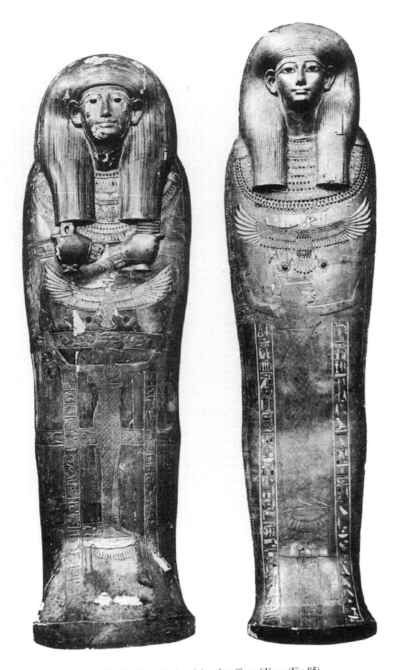

The lids of the third and fourth coffins of Yuya (Fig 85)

The Fourth Coffin: Cairo Museum Catalogue Number **51004.**
Exhibition Number **3669.**

The last of Yuya's coffins is entirely covered in gold leaf. The necklace, vulture and two columns of text are of coloured inlay with the remaining decoration executed in delicate low relief.

The inside of both the lid and base is covered in silver, incised with inscriptions and reliefs.

As with the other coffins, the eyes are inlaid, but have an additional feature, with the corners of the eyes having a touch of red paint.

On the foot of the lid is a relief of the Goddess Isis.

The gold is laid on a thin layer of plaster, which has been backed with cloth. This plaster coating has suffered from rough treatment at the time the tomb was robbed in antiquity and it is now very fragile. Where fragments have fallen away, the carved designs are revealed on the wood.

The coffin shows many signs of alterations in ancient times. The name of Yuya on the outside of the lid is of a slightly different coloured gold to the rest of the coffin and has perhaps been patched on to replace another name. Alternatively, the coffin may have been made with no particular prospective owner in mind, only to have the details inserted when Yuya decided that he wanted this coffin.

Length of the coffin 2.04 metres. Breadth 0.55 metres.
Height 0.59 metres.

This fourth coffin contained the wrapped mummy of Yuya. Over the head and upper part of the body was a funeral mask (Cairo Museum Catalogue Number **51008**) made of plaster and gilded, with features similar to the fourth coffin. The inside is painted with black pitch.

This mask was badly damaged by the robbers when they ripped the bandages off to get at any jewellery on the body.

The chin and the right side of the head of the mask are broken.

Length of the mask 0.33 metres. Breadth 0.41 metres.

A series of bands (Cairo Museum Catalogue Number **51010**) made of cloth plastered and gilded enclosed the mummy similar to the bands shown on the second coffin, keeping the bandages in place. Both the vertical and transverse bands are inscribed.

Note. The mask and bands are not illustrated.

THUYA.

The Mummy: Cairo Museum Catalogue Number **51191**.

Like the mummy of her husband, the wrappings of the mummy of Thuya have been severely damaged by robbers.

The bandages have been covered in black resin, which still bear the impressions of stolen jewellery.

The mummy presents some unusual features for the period.

The embalming incision is almost vertical and has been sewn up with string. No plate covers the wound, which gapes open, exposing the linen packing filling the body cavity.

The arms are fully extended with the palms of the hands flattened against the thighs.

The mummy is of a small old lady, with typical Egyptian features, who was possibly over fifty when she died.

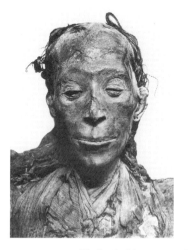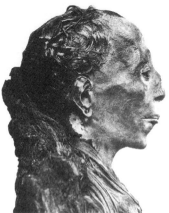

The head of the mummy of Thuya (Figs 86 and 87)

112

Thuya has scanty white hair, now turned yellow by the materials used in the embalming. On the top of her head the hair is very thin and is about the same length as her husband's. (What looks very much like a 'pony tail' in photographs, are in fact, the remains of the linen wrappings around the head and back of the neck of the mummy).

The nostrils have been packed with resin and the nose has been flattened by the pressure of the bandages. Both ears have double piercing for ear-rings.

Packing has also been introduced into the eye sockets and has been painted to represent the pupils of the eyes.

The internal organs have been removed from the body and were placed in a canopic chest which was also found in the tomb.

X-Rays show that Thuya suffered from arthritis in her old age and that no attempt was made by the embalmers to remove the brains.

Height of the body 1.496 metres.

The Coffins:

The Sledge-Canopy.   Cairo Museum Catalogue Number **51005**.
                           Exhibition Number **3705**.

The sledge-canopy of Thuya is similar to the sledge-canopy of Yuya, but it is smaller and is a complete box with a floor.

Made of wood it is painted with black pitch with gilt plaster decoration. The reliefs are much better executed than those of Yuya.

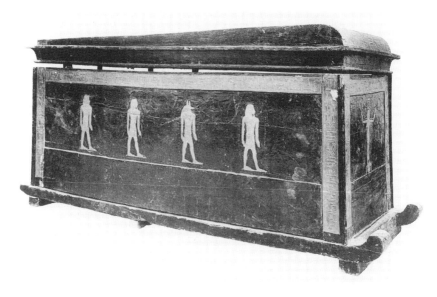

The sledge-canopy of Thuya (Fig 88)

To reach the coffins and mummy contained in this first coffin, the robbers detached one side of the box, but did not otherwise damage it.

Unlike the sledge of Yuya, this sledge could not have been pulled along the ground for two horizontal blocks of wood are fixed underneath and across the runners.

Total length, including the sledge 2.79 metres. Length of the coffin 2.49 metres. Breadth 1.04 metres. Height 1.30 metres.

The Second Coffin: Cairo Museum Catalogue Number **51006.** Exhibition Number **3704.**

The best preserved of all the coffins from the tomb, the second coffin of Thuya is entirely covered in gold, except for the inlaid eyes and necklace. The gold is blotched in many places with patches of what looks like red rust (probably some impurities in the gold).

All the other decoration on the coffin is in low relief. Above the forehead is a small figure of the Goddess Nephthys. She is shown with raised arms and kneeling on a 'neb' sign. The figure of the Goddess Isis appears on the soles of the feet of the coffin.

The hands of the coffin are crossed over the chest and hold no symbols.

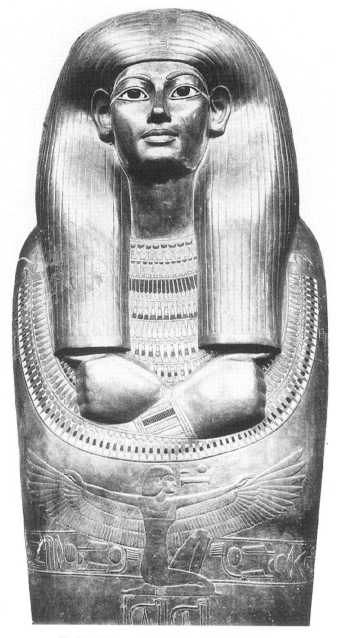

The lid of the second coffin of Thuya (detail) (Fig 89)

Length of the coffin 2.185 metres. Breadth 0.66 metres. Height 0.94 metres.

The Third Coffin: Cairo Museum Catalogue Number **51007.**
Exhibition Number **3671.**

The exterior of the final coffin of Thuya is also entirely covered in gold, with the decoration in low relief. The eyes are inlaid, as is the pectoral.

   The interior is covered in silver, but is devoid of any inscriptions or reliefs. Part of the gilt mask which covered the head of the mummy still adheres to the inside of the coffin, as do some pieces of the mummy wrappings.

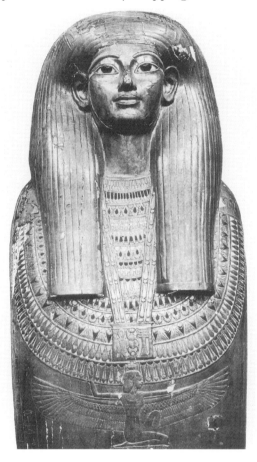

The lid of the third coffin of Thuya (detail) (Fig 90)

   Many parts of the gilt plaster are lost especially around the head.

Length of the coffin 1.945 metres. Breadth 0.53 metres.
Height 0.65 metres.

The Gilt Mask Cairo Museum Catalogue Number 51009.
Exhibition Number 3685.

Made of linen which has been coated with plaster, the mask is covered with gold into which are inlaid eyes and a broad collar. A floral fillet encircles the head.

The face and front of the mask was covered by a fine linen cloth at the time of the burial. Over the centuries the linen has carbonised and adhered to the surface of the mask, giving the appearance of a veil. The early photographs of the mask clearly show the material covering the finely modelled features.

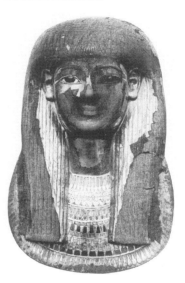

The gilt mask of Thuya (Fig 91)

In 1982 the mask was cleaned and restored in the Cairo Museum and the material adhering to the face and head was removed (although some was left on parts of the wig).

Height of the mask 0.40 metres. Breadth 0.28 metres.

An open-work cloth and gilt plaster sheath, 1.21 metres in length and 0.25 metres wide covered the front of the mummy.

The sheath is essentially composed of straps holding the bandages in place. The spaces between the straps are filled with figures of the Gods, so that the result is rather like a cage. The surface is covered with inscriptions in relief.

Note: This sheath (Cairo Museum Catalogue number 51011) is not illustrated.

AMENHOTEP III.   18th Dynasty.   1386-1349 B.C.

Son of Thutmose IV and Queen Mutemuia, Amenhotep married Tiye, daughter of Yuya and Thuya (whose tomb was discovered in the Valley of the Kings). He was a great builder and added extensively to the temples at Karnak and Luxor. He built a large funerary temple on the west bank of the Nile at Thebes. Only two colossal statues survive today, known to us as the Colosssi of Memnon. Original tomb in the Valley of the Kings, number 22.

The Mummy: Found in the tomb of Amenhotep II in 1898.
Cairo Museum Catalogue Number **61074**.
Exhibition Number **6349A**.

The priests of the 21st Dynasty had written the names of Amenhotep III on both the coffins and the wrappings of the mummy. The wrappings were removed by Elliot Smith on September 23rd 1905.

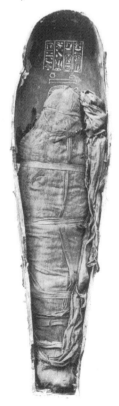

*The wrapped mummy and base
of the coffin of Amenhotep III
(Fig 92)*

118

Elliot Smith revealed a severely damaged mummy, perhaps the worst of all the Royal mummies. The head has been broken off, the front part of the body is missing and all the limbs are damaged. Virtually no soft tissue remains on the body.

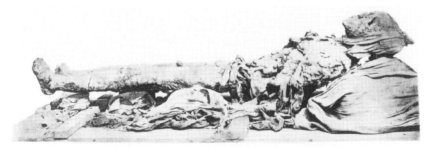

The mummy of Amenhotep III, partly unwrapped (Fig 93)

Elliot Smith had difficulty in estimating the age of the King at death; he thought between forty and fifty. Clear X-Rays were difficult to obtain because of the method of embalming, but the Michigan team decided that fifty would appear to be more likely.

The mummy shows that Amenhotep was probably obese at his death. The embalmers used a new technique when preparing the body. They packed a resinous paste and pieces of linen beneath the skin. This was moulded into shape in an attempt to restore a lifelike appearance.

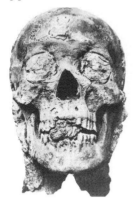 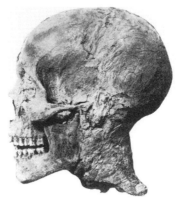

The head of the mummy of Amenhotep III (Figs 94 and 95)

The teeth are particularly bad and the King must have been in considerable pain at times during his last years, from alveolar abscesses.

Height of the body 1.561 metres

The Coffin: Cairo Museum Catalogue Number **61036.**

This coffin is of crude workmanship. The coffin lid bears both the names of Seti II and Amenhotep III, whose body it contained.

The base of the coffin bears the name of Ramesses III.

This multiple inscription illustrates well the state of chaos and confusion faced by the restorers of the Royal burials, with bodies and coffins separated. Small wonder that the correct identification of some of the mummies is in doubt.

This coffin was made in the 20th Dynasty. It had been damaged before being used for the re-burial of the King and the original decoration over a layer of plaster has been lost.

When re-used the coffin was given a coat of white paint and a brief inscription added in black painted hieroglyphs and hieratic.

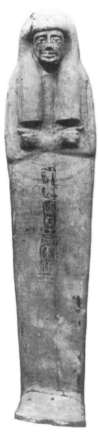

The lid of the coffin of Amenhotep III (Fig 96)

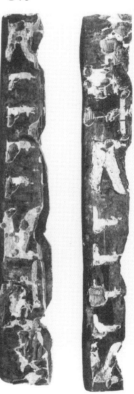

The base of the coffin bearing the name of Ramesses III which held the mummy of Amenhotep III (Fig 97)

Length of the coffin 1.82 metres. Breadth 0.45 metres. Height 0.31 metres.

QUEEN TIYE.　　　　18th Dynasty.　　　c 1340 B.C.

Queen Tiye was the principal Royal Wife of Amenhotep III and was the daughter of non-Royal parents, Yuya and Thuya.

The Mummy:　　Found in the tomb of Amenhotep II in 1898.
　　　　　　　　Cairo Museum Catalogue Number **61070**.

This mummy was found in a side-chamber of the tomb of Amenhotep II, along with two other mummies, one female and one male.

　　It was known simply as the 'Elder Woman', as the 21st Dynasty priests had left no indication as to the identity of the body.

　　Elliot Smith dated the body to the 18th Dynasty by the mummification techniques.

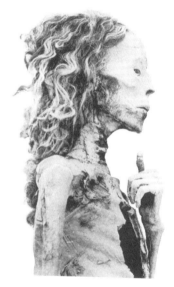 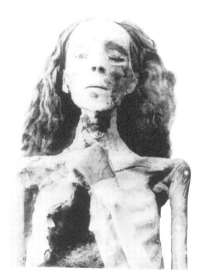

The mummy of Queen Tiye (Detail) (Figs 98 and 99)

　　The body is of a middle aged woman, with long, naturally curled, dark brown hair some thirty centimetres long, parted in the centre of the head.

　　The features of the face are fine and pointed. The teeth are well worn.

This body, too, has suffered badly at the hands of the tomb robbers, for the whole of the front of the abdomen has been broken away. The right arm is extended, with the left folded over the chest. The position of the left arm has in the past been considered by some as 'royal' and the mummy had been tentatively identified as that of Queen Hatshepsut.

In 1976, the Michigan team took X-Rays of the body and concluded from these that the features exhibited fitted in well with those that Tiye could have inherited from her known ancestors. The mummies of both Tiye's parents survive and were also examined by the team.

The team then approached the Egyptian authorities and asked for permission to use some hairs from a locket found in Tutankhamun's tomb, which bore an inscription saying that the hair belonged to Queen Tiye. Using a device known as an electron probe, they tested these hairs and found that they were identical to those on the head of the mummy. This evidence is considered to be quite convincing, since hair is as peculiar to a person as fingerprints.

Even this 'positive' identification has, however, recently been questioned.

Some now identify this as the body of Ankhesenamun, Queen of Tutankaumun.

Once again, only further detailed scientific analysis will answer all the questions and convince the sceptical.

No coffin was found with this mummy, which still lies in the side chamber in the tomb of Amenhotep II.

Height of the body 1.455 metres.

SMENKHKARE.   18th Dynasty.   1336-1334 B.C.

Smenkhkare was possibly a son of Amenhotep III and brother of Tutankhamun. He married Meritaten, one of the daughters of Akhenaten and on her death married Ankhesenpaaten another daughter and also wife to Akhenaten. It is possible that Smenkhkare ruled jointly as Co-Regent with Akhenaten and as sole ruler for a short while after Akhenaten's death.

The uncertainty about the complex family relationships of

this period have filled several large volumes with theories on who was related to whom. Many of these problems will only be resolved when all the surviving mummies of this particular family group have been examined more fully.

The Tomb: KV 55.

Discovered by Edward Ayrton in January 1907, this tomb has proved to be one of the most problematic finds in the Valley of the Kings.

Only scanty records of the excavation were kept. With many of the objects being in an extremely fragmentary and fragile state, much information which might have been available at the time of the discovery has been lost to us.

It would appear that this tomb was used as a cache for some of the Royal burials which were moved to Thebes when Akhenaten's city of Akhetaten was abandoned.

Many of the contents were made for Queen Tiye, notably the large remains of a dismantled gilt-wooden shrine.

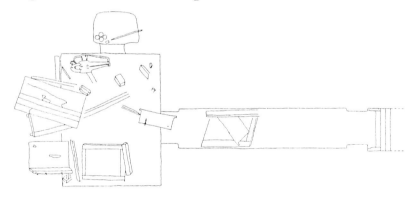

Plan of tomb KV 55. (Fig 100)

It is evident that at some stage the burial of Queen Tiye was removed from the tomb and taken elsewhere, leaving behind the shrine, along with a coffined body (from which all the names had deliberately been erased) and various other items of funerary equipment. The identity of this body has been a matter of great speculation and debate ever since.

The location of the body can be seen in the above plan of the tomb. It was lying in a corner of the large burial chamber and adjacent to a small recess (the beginnings of an unfinished second chamber) which contained four uninscribed alabaster canopic jars.

The remains of the Gilt Shrine were scattered around the burial chamber and in the entrance corridor. These dismantled panels were in the process of being removed from the tomb, but insufficient blocking material had been removed from the entrance to allow them to pass through. In what must have been a hasty operation the pieces were abandoned.

The Mummy: Found in January 1907 by Theodore M. Davis in the Valley of the Kings. Tomb number **55**.
Cairo Museum Catalogue Number **61075**.
Exhibition Number **6349B**.

From the moment of discovery, the identity of this mummy has been the subject of great debate. The excavation of the tomb was badly conducted and much valuable information was lost. The tomb had been plundered in antiquity and was in an extreme state of disorder. To make matters worse, water had entered the tomb and most of the wooden items which survived were in an extremely delicate state and fell apart when touched.

Davis identified the body as that of a female and as Queen Tiye, because of some objects in the tomb which bore her name. Elliot Smith showed that the body was in fact that of a male, aged between twenty-five and twenty-six.

The assumption at this time was that the mummy must be that of Akhenaten.

Little more than the skeleton remains. The bad condition of the body on this occasion was caused by the dampness of the tomb, rather than by the actions of tomb robbers.

Joseph Linden Smith, who was present at the opening of the tomb, unwrapped the mummy in the tomb. He recorded that the left arm was bent with the hand on the breast, with the right arm laying by the side of the body, with the hand resting on the thigh. This position is assumed to be peculiar to female Royal mummies and is certainly unusual, if not unique for a male mummy. Once unwrapped, the bones were packed into a box for shipment to Cairo. Only a disarticulated skeleton remained for a more detailed study.

Several items of gold remained on the body, but all traces of inscriptions which would have identified the body had been deliberately removed in antiquity.

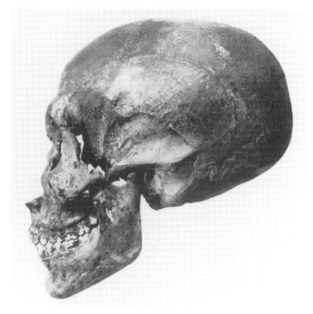

The head of the mummy of Smenkhkare (Fig 101)

Arthur Weigall, at the time of the discovery, did note some gold bands, which bore the name of Akhenaten, but these disappeared soon afterwards and were not included in the excavation report. It is beleived that these have been found in recent years in a private collection.

The body was then 'identified' as that of King Akhenaten (1350-1334 B.C.).

Much research over the last few years has discounted this theory and opinion today is that it is Smenkhkare.

A more recent examination of the skeleton has, however, produced an estimated age at death of thirty to thirty-five years, which re-introduces the possibility that this mummy might, after all, be that of Akhenaten.

Examination of the skeletal remains has shown a marked similarity to Tutankhamun and it is more than likely that they were brothers. There is some skeletal resemblance to earlier members of the family, although the loss of some parts of the skeleton when it was moved from Luxor to Cairo may have destroyed some important evidence.

The Coffin: Cairo Museum Exhibition Number 3873.

The coffin found in tomb 55 is extremely elaborate; made of wood, it is overlaid with gold and inlaid with hundreds of pieces of coloured glass paste. No such coffin had been found before. The wood was in a poor state of preservation and conservation of this unique piece was difficult. The coffin was split from end to end and the base had virtually rotted away because of water in the tomb. Only the coffin lid is on display in the Cairo Museum today.

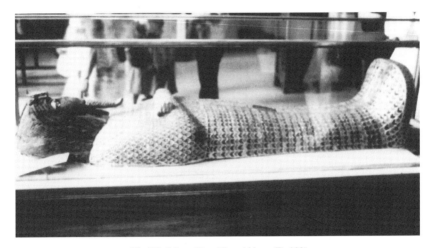

The lid of the coffin of Smenkhkare (Fig102)

Almost as much controversy surrounds this coffin as surrounds the mummy it contained. It would appear to have been made for a Royal female burial, it is believed for Queen Kiya, a wife of Akhenaten. The shape of the wig is particularly feminine in design. It is evident that the coffin was adapted for the burial of a King by the addition of the Royal Cobra on the brow and the Royal Beard. An inlaid inscription runs down the centre of the coffin, but the all-important name has been removed.

*The face of the coffin of Smenkhkare
(Fig 103)*

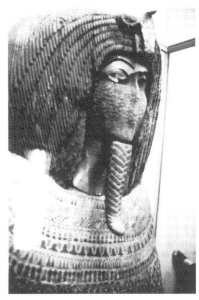

A mask of heavy gold once covered the wooden face, but this has been ripped away at some time, leaving only pieces at the neck and forehead. The wooden face is greatly decayed.

*Detail of the decoration and
inscription of the coffin of Smenkhkare
showing the erased name (Fig 104)*

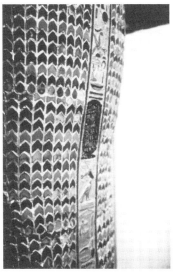

The head of the coffin appears not to have originally belonged to the body of the coffin and may have been cut from another coffin and joined to the body of the 'new' coffin.

The interior of the coffin was lined with heavy sheets of gold which had become detached and fallen over the mummy.

The hands of the coffin once held the symbols of Royalty, the Crook and the Flail, but only some fragments of the Flail have survived

It is thought that after Akhenaten's new Capital city, Akhetaten (modern Tell el Amarna) was abandoned, the Royal burials made there were moved to Thebes. The memory of Akhenaten was officially erased from all records and monuments and the mummy, possibly thought to be that of Akhenaten was re-buried in an unmarked coffin and left to oblivion.

TUTANKHAMUN.   18th Dynasty.   1334-1325 B.C.

Possibly a son of Amenhotep III, Tutankhamun was born during the reign of Akhenaten and was a follower of the cult of the God Aten. He changed his name to Tutankh*amun* from Tutankh*aten* upon his becoming King, when he re-introduced the worship of the old Gods and moved the capital of Egypt from Akhenaten's city at Amarna, back to Thebes.

He died at a relatively young age and was buried in the Valley of the Kings, where his virtually intact tomb (number 62) was discovered in 1922 by Howard Carter and Lord Carnarvon.

The Tomb: KV 62.

The story of this tomb, discovered by Howard Carter and Lord Carnarvon in November 1922, is well known. Situated in the floor of the Valley of the Kings, the location of this tomb was soon lost; the building of the tomb of Ramesses VI almost directly above further ensured that the tomb remained undiscovered.

The tomb was robbed on at least two occasions, which must have been relatively soon after the burial. The tomb was hastily tidied by the Necropolis Priests and re-sealed.

A small tomb by Valley standards, it was probably not originally intended for the burial of the King. Upon the possibly unexpected and early death of the King, this tomb was pressed into service and was hastily completed to receive the burial.

The robbers had not managed to break into the four gilt shrines surrounding the Sarcophagus. The body of the King was, therefore, found completely intact, just as it had been laid to rest on the day of his funeral.

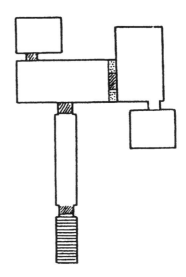

Plan of the tomb of Tutankhamun.
(Fig 105)

The Mummy: Still buried in his third mummiform coffin, in his own tomb in the Valley of the Kings. Tomb Number **62.**

Although the tomb of Tutankhamun had been plundered by robbers, on at least two separate occasions, it still contained great treasures, the likes of which had never been found before by Egyptologists. Most important of all, the burial chamber was completely intact; Carter established at an early stage, that the original seals were still in place on the gilt wooden shrines which covered the sarcophagus.

He would have been well aware of the fine state of preservation of some of the Royal mummies discovered earlier. There was every reason, therefore, to expect that the mummy of Tutankhamun would prove to be the best preserved of all, having been undisturbed by robbers.

It is a supreme irony that exactly the opposite proved to be the case.

As Carter opened the coffins containing the mummy, he found evidence of humidity and that the coffins must have been sealed before the mummy was dry.

When revealed, the body was found to be completely enclosed in bandages, which were dark and brittle. The body was firmly stuck to the mummiform coffin by the libations poured over the mummy at the time of burial, which had set solid. Carter estimated that virtually a bucket and a half had been poured over the mummy.

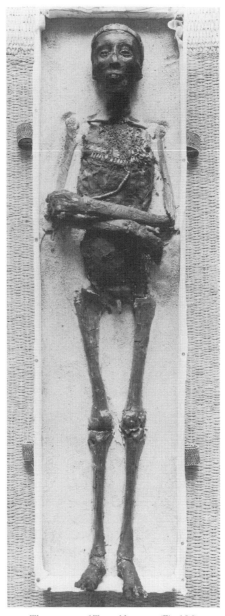

The mummy of Tutankhamun. (Fig 106)

The bandages were consolidated with melted paraffin wax and removed in large pieces. Each layer revealed items of jewellery, which covered the body from head to foot.

A detailed examination of the body was made by two doctors, Douglas E. Derry and Saleh Bey Hamdin. This examination was made with the body still in the coffin. A further study of the body was made more recently in 1968 when X-Rays were taken, although this examination also had to be made within the confines of the tomb.

The skin of the mummy is a grey-white colour. It is very brittle and is cracked. The liquids poured over the body, caused carbonisation of the soft tissue, by means of a kind of spontaneous combustion due to the heat and humidity within the coffins.

Carter experienced great difficulty in actually extracting the body from the gold mask and the shell of the mummiform coffin as it was firmly embedded in the rock-hard resin. Exposure to the heat of the sun failed to soften the resin and separate the mask and coffin. This process may have damaged the mummy and the carbonisation of the soft tissue of the body may well have occurred at this stage, before the body was properly unwrapped and not, as Carter suggested as a result of liquid unguents poured over the mummy.

The options available to Carter were somewhat limited; leave the body intact (and all the objects *in situ*) or remove the objects the best way he could. Damage to the body was inevitable and the body was effectively removed piece by piece from the coffin. This process exposed some of the bones, enabling medical evidence to be obtained on the age of the King at his death, which was estimated to be 18 years. X-Rays have since confirmed this age.

Some of the photographs taken at the time and used in *The Tomb of Tutankhamen* by Carter and Mace, do not show the damage to the body. Other photographs for the main archaeological records clearly show that the body was disarticulated. Head, limbs, hands and feet were all broken from the body in the process of removing it from the coffin.

Some damage is particularly obvious; the first photographs of the head show the ears clearly; later photographs taken by Burton, show damaged ears. The damage was probably caused whilst removing a gold band from the head. More damage has occurred in the intervening years and the most recent photographs taken of the mummy reveal that the ears are now virtually missing. Other parts of the body appear to be missing, including the penis, which is clearly visible in the first photographs.

The head, fingers and toes of the mummy are slightly better preserved, as all were enclosed in gold and were not, therefore,

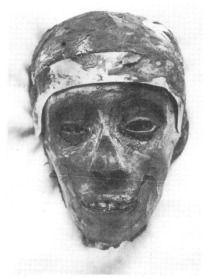
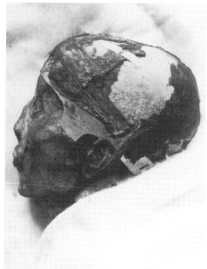

The head of the mummy of Tutankhamun (Figs 107 and 108)

in direct contact with the liquid unguents.

When finally revealed, the head was found to be clean shaven.

The nostrils have been plugged with linen, impregnated with resin. The eyes are partly open. Pressure from the bandages, has partly flattened the soft tissues of the nose. The head is broad and flat-topped similar to representations of the King and members of the family of Akhenaten, in reliefs and sculpture.

The height of the King when alive is estimated to have been 1.676 metres.

The cause of the King's death was not apparent to Carter, who was not able to X-Ray the body. Much is made about a rounded depression on the left cheek, just in front of the ear lobe. The skin filling the depression resembles a scab and the area around it appears to be discoloured. It is not known how this was caused, or if it contributed in any way to the death of the King.

Carter stated that the mummy was re-wrapped before being re-interred. The body was re-assembled in a shallow tray of sand, which enabled it to be restored to some semblance of order.

The 're-wrapping' simply consisted of covering the tray with pads of material. The more recent examinations have dislodged parts of the body which still remain on this tray within the outer mummiform coffin. Carter would have had real difficulties in actually re-wrapping the damaged mummy, a problem encountered by the priests who restored some of the other Royal burials and who had to resort to bandaging the bodies to planks of wood.

Modern techniques of non-destructive investigation would leave most mummies undisturbed and this has been the case with many more recent discoveries. If, however, a similar Royal mummy, covered in objects of both artistic and intrinsic value, was discovered today, it is more than likely that curiosity and the desire to reveal and display the possibly unique objects would win the day. Some damage would be inevitable, as removing inflexible and fragile objects from an inflexible and fragile body will never be an easy task.

It is apparent that the mummy of the King has been allowed to deteriorate over the last seventy years, when the other Royal mummies have been looked after well by comparison. One obvious example of the deterioration is that the body is now much darker in colour than when first revealed. It is ironic that the cause of this deterioration may have been the decision to leave the body in the tomb in far from ideal conditions. To date, no efforts appear to have been made to ensure that further deterioration does not occur.

There has been much speculation on the the cause of death.

The X-Rays revealed an unusual feature of the mummy, in that some of the ribs of the chest and the sternum are missing. Carter did not notice this because of the hard resin covering the mummy. These bones are unlikely to have been removed as part of the embalming process. Dennis Forbes Editor of *KMT* magazine (A modern Journal of Ancient Egypt) has proposed a theory that the King was involved in some form of accident, such as falling from a chariot, which effectively caved in his chest.

The Coffins:

Some of the Royal coffins previously discovered, gave an indication as to how elaborate they originally were, even though virtually all of them had been damaged or defaced in some way.

With the discovery of Tutankhamun's tomb, three intact Royal coffins were found. Each rested within the other, like a set of Russian dolls. The space between the coffins was only the width of a finger in places. The coffins were enclosed in turn, in a pink quartzite sarcophagus which was itself enclosed in four gilt wooden shrines.

The Third Mummiform coffin:

Although this was the first coffin to be revealed, it is in fact the third coffin, numbering from the mummy outwards.

When the sarcophagus was first opened, the coffin was covered by a fine linen shroud, which was a dark brown in colour.

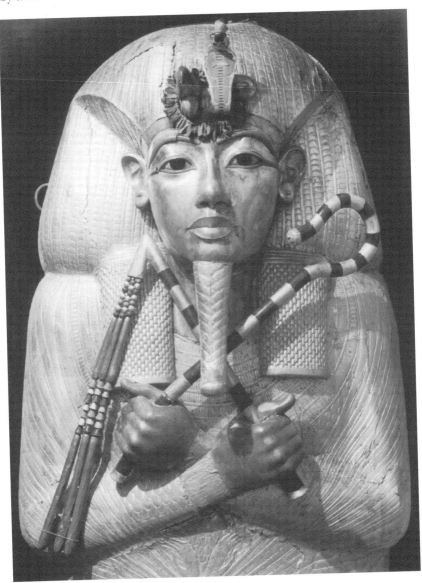

The lid of the third coffin of Tutankhamun (detail) (Fig 109)

The coffin is of wood which has been overlaid with a coating of thin plaster and gilded. It is anthropoid in shape and shows the King wearing the Khat head-dress. The face and hands are covered with heavier gold.

The traditional 'rishi' feather decoration is used which has been incised into the gold. The King holds the Crook and Flail. A deep blue glass paste is used to inlay the insignia and also the eyes, eyebrows and the Cobra and Vulture on the King's brow.

The lid was fixed to the coffin base by ten silver tongues which fitted into corresponding sockets in the thickness of the shell, where they were secured by substantial gold-headed silver pins.

This coffin still lies within the sarcophagus in the King's tomb and contains the mummy of Tutankhamun - the only Pharaoh to remain in his tomb.

Length of the coffin 2.235 metres.

The Second Mummiform coffin: Cairo Museum Exhibition
                                    Number 222.

Lying within the third coffin, this coffin was also covered by a linen shroud, much decayed. Upon this shroud floral garlands had been placed, composed of olive and willow leaves, petals of the blue lotus and cornflower. The coffin revealed was far more elaborate than the third and is similar in design to the coffin of Smenkhkare.

Made of wood which has been gilded, it is inlaid with coloured glass paste and semi-precious stones. This inlay is in the familiar 'rishi' design. The two Royal animals, the Cobra and Vulture, spread their wings around the body of the King.

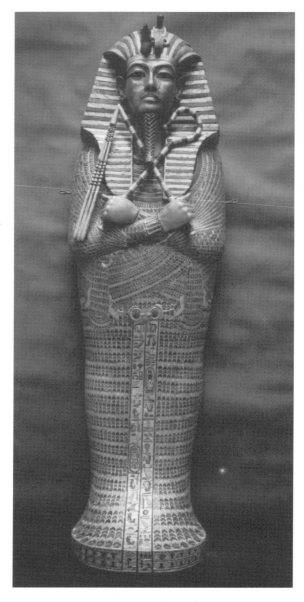

The lid of the second coffin of Tutankhamun (Fig 110)

Once again the coffin depicts the mummified figure of the King holding the Royal insignia. The King wears the Nemset headdress and the wide collar and beard of the Gods.

The face and hands of the coffin are covered by a thicker layer of gold than the rest of the coffin.

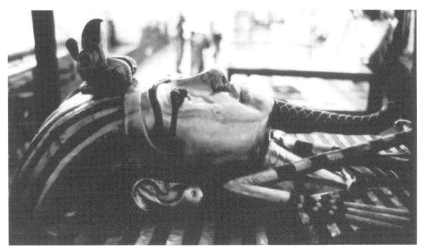

The face of the second coffin of Tutankhamun (Fig 111)

The preservation of this coffin caused Carter great problems, for the wood had become fragile because of the humidity within the coffins. This caused the plaster and gilded surface to become detached in places from the wood and the pieces of inlay, set in plaster, had become loose.

The features of this coffin differ significantly from those of the first and third coffins and also from other known representations of the King. This has led to the belief that this coffin was not originally made for the King. There are many objects from the tomb which Tutankhamun appears to have inherited or usurped which have altered inscriptions.

Length of the coffin, 2.032 metres. Breadth 0.685 metres. Height 0.787 metres.

The Mummiform Coffin: Cairo Museum Exhibition Number 219.

Carter could not understand why the mummy enclosed in the three coffins was so heavy. (It took eight men to lift the coffins). The weight did not lessen significantly when the third coffin was removed.

When the second coffin was opened, another shrouded coffin was revealed. Carter rolled back the shroud and was amazed to find that the mummiform coffin was made of solid gold. Garlands of natural leaves and flowers had been placed on the coffin at the time of burial.

The King is again shown as a mummy, wearing the Nemset head-dress. The coffin is decorated with inlays of coloured glass paste and semi-precious stones and the gold has been incised with the 'rishi' design and the figures of protective Goddesses, who spread their protective wings around the body.

The eyes of the coffin are missing, as the white calcite had decayed and crumbled away. Remains of the eyes are visible on the first photographs of the coffin before it was fully excavated and cleaned.

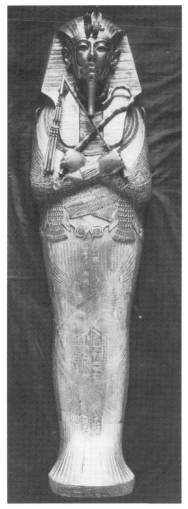

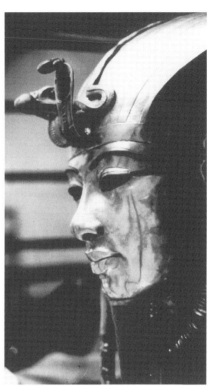

The face of the first coffin of Tutankhamun (Fig 113)

The lid of the first coffin of Tutankhamun (Fig 112)

Length of the coffin. 1.879 metres. Breadth. 0.508 metres. Height, 0.508 metres.

The Funeral Mask.   Cairo Museum Exhibition Number **220.**

When the gold mummiform coffin was opened, the mummy of the King was finally revealed. In appearance, it resembled the three coffins, for a solid gold portrait mask covered the top of the body. Gold hands had been sewn to the outer bandages and these held the Crook and the Flail. One heavy inlaid gold band ran lengthways down the body and three horizontally, to hold the bandages in place.

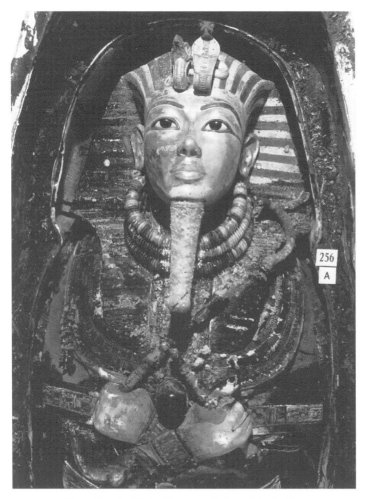

The gold mask of Tutankhamun as first revealed (Fig 114)

The mask is the finest ever found and shows workmanship of the highest order. It was placed immediately on the bandaged

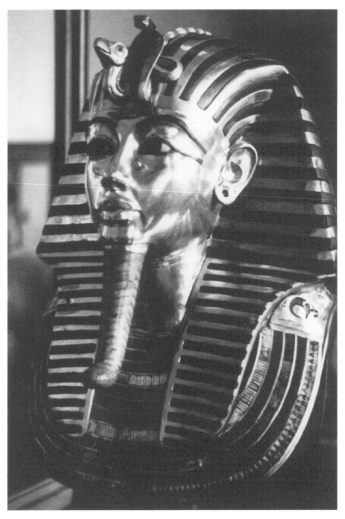

The gold mask of Tutankhamun in the Cairo Museum (Fig 115)

face of the King and is lifesize. Made of beaten gold, it is inlaid with coloured glass paste and semi-precious stones. The King is shown wearing the Nemset head-dress, a broad collar and the beard of the Gods. When found, a triple string of round flat beads covered the neck of the mask.

The ears are pierced, but when discovered the holes were covered with discs of thin gold.

Height of the mask, 0.533 metres . Width at the shoulders, 0.394 metres.

TWO INFANT BURIALS FROM THE TOMB OF TUTANKHAMUN. 18th Dynasty. C. 1320 B. C.

The Mummies: Found in the 'Treasury' of the tomb of Tutankhamun in 1922. Tomb Catalogue Numbers 317a2 and 317b2.

317a2.

This is the body of a prematurely born child, probably female. The skin is of a greyish colour, very shrunken and brittle with the ribs clearly showing through. The skin has been pressed into folds on the limbs following the desiccation of the tissue. The bones of the hands are clearly defined. The arms are extended with the hands resting on the thighs.

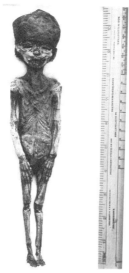

Foetus 317a2 : tomb of Tutankhamun (Fig 116)

There is no embalming incision; with such a small body the embalmers obviously considered evisceration unnecessary.

The age of the foetus is estimated at about four months development.

Height of the body 0.2575 metres.

The whereabouts of this mummy today is not known, although the mummy of the second foetus has been re-discovered in the University of Cairo.

141

317b2.

This is the body of a prematurely born child, also probably female. This body is in a similar condition to the first foetus, but the hands are placed beside the thighs.

The eyelids are open with the sockets containing no packing. Some packing material has been inserted into the cranial cavity.

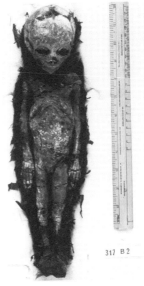

Foetus 317b2 : tomb of Tutankhamun (Fig 117)

There is an embalming incision in the abdominal wall and the cavity has been packed with linen.

The age of development of the foetus is estimated at seven or eight months.

X-Rays of this foetus, taken in 1979, show multiple skeletal anomalies which include scoloisis, spina bifida and an inheritable condition known as Sprengel's deformity (upward displacement of the scapula, in this case the left). If Tutankhamun and Ankhesenamun were the parents of this child, perhaps the end of the 18th Dynasty royal blood-line owes much more to inheritance than to misfortune.

Height of the body 0.395 metres.

There is no clue at all in the tomb as to the identification of the bodies, who are assumed to be still-born children of Tutankhamun and Ankhesenamum. It was not uncommon at this time for infant burials to be included in their parents' tomb.

The Coffins: Tomb Catalogue Numbers 317a/317a1 and
317b/317b1. Cairo Museum
Exhibition Numbers 956-964.

Both sets of coffins were found in an undecorated wooden chest, the lid of which had been removed in antiquity. The coffins lay head to foot in the box.

The toes of coffin 317b have been hacked away to allow the lid of the box to close.

Two straps of linen had been tied around each coffin, to which was attached the clay seal of the Theban Necropolis.

Both the outer coffins are of black painted wood with the decoration detailed in gold over a layer of plaster. Brief inscriptions on the coffins give no clues as to the identity of their occupants.

Contained within each of these coffins was a second. Made of wood, both second coffins are covered in plaster and gilded. The wrapped mummies were found within these gilt coffins.

The mummy in 317a had a gilt cartonnage funeral mask placed over it. The mask was far too large for the small body. A second mask, possibly intended for the other body (but too small for it) was found in tomb KV 54 along with various embalming debris, in 1907.

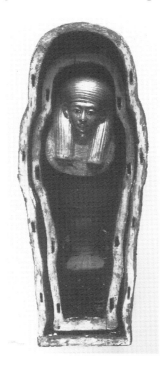

The bases of coffins 317a and 317a1 containing the wrapped foetus and funeral mask. (Fig 118)

143

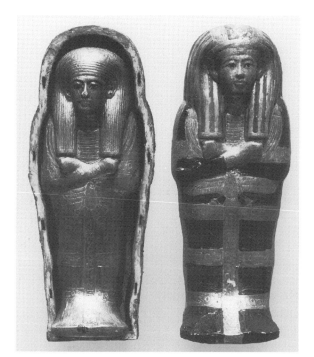

*Coffins 317a1: and 317a
tomb of Tutankhamun
(Fig 119)*

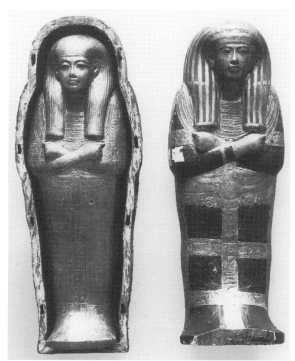

*Coffins 317b1 and 317b:
tomb of Tutankhamun
(Fig 120)*

144

NEBSENI.   18th Dynasty.   Date uncertain.

Little is known about Nebseni, other than the fact that he was a priest and scribe.

The Mummy: Found in the Royal Cache at Deir el Bahri in 1881.
Cairo Museum Catalogue Number **61067.**

This mummy is identified as being that of Nebseni, as it was found in a coffin bearing this name. Unlike many of the mummies which

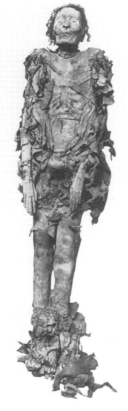

*The mummy of Nebseni
(Fig 121)*

had dockets attached to the wrappings identifing the individuals, this body bore no name. In the absence of any other information, this identification cannot either be proved or disproved. It is evident that other coffins and mummies found in the Cache often bear no relation to each other.

The unwrapped body is intact although it had been disturbed by robbers and re-wrapped by Priests in the 21st Dynasty.

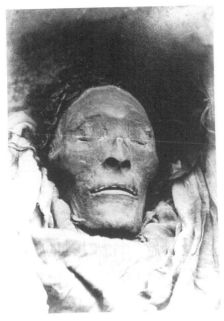

The head of the mummy of Nebseni (Fig 122)

This photograph was taken with the mummy only partly unwrapped and whilst it still lay in the coffin.

This mummy of a minor and otherwise unknown individual has not been given the full examination accorded to the better known mummies.

Height of the body 1.739 metres.

The Coffin: Cairo Museum Catalogue Number **61016.**

The mummy known as Nebseni was found in an anthropoid cedar coffin, bearing that name.

The bottom of the base is carved out of the trunk of a tree with planks added to raise the height of the sides. The lid is also carved from one block with added planks at the sides. The feet of the coffin are missing.

The arms are crossed over the chest with the hands painted yellow, as is the face. The head-dress is painted in blue and yellow stripes and there is a multi-coloured painted collar. The rest of the coffin is painted white with yellow bands of inscriptions.

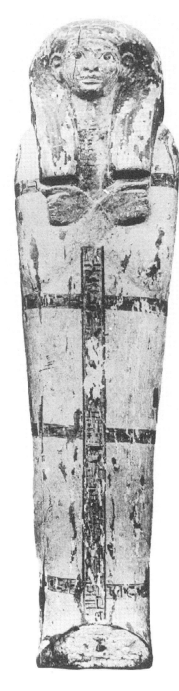

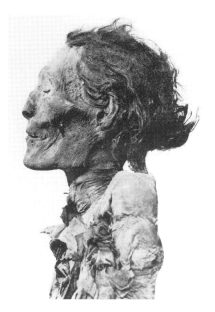

The head of the mummy of Nebseni (Fig 123)

The lid of the coffin of Nebseni (Fig 124)

Length of the coffin 1.97 metres. Breadth 0.525 metres.
Height 0.63 metres.

UNKNOWN MAN   18th Dynasty.   Date Uncertain.

The Mummy: Found in the Royal Cache at Deir el Bahri in 1881.
Cairo Museum Catalogue Number **61098.**

This mummy, unwrapped on June 30th 1886, was found in a plain white, uninscribed, coffin.

The body is that of a young man. The arms are extended and the hands are placed near to each other, but not touching, in front of the pubes.

No attempt has been made to compose the features of the mummy or to put the head into the usual position. The head is thrown back and set obliquely on the neck, with the mouth wide open.

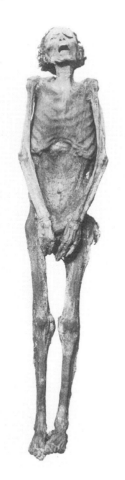

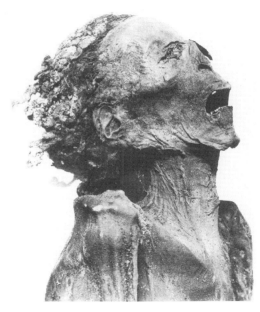

The mummy of an Unknown Man (detail)
(Fig 126)

The mummy of an Unknown Man (Fig 125)

The hair is plaited, the ears pierced and the teeth are only slightly worn. There is no sign of any beard or moustache and the genitals are absent.

There is a cheese-like material on the hair and the skin of the face has formed ridges, like those on the mummy of Ahmose-Inhapi.

There is no embalming incision and this body has been treated differently from all other New Kingdom mummies.

Dating the mummy is difficult but Elliot Smith considered it to be of the Eighteenth Dynasty.

Various ideas have been put forward to explain the attitude of the body, including poisoning and burial whilst still alive. Elliot Smith points out that there is absolutely no evidence to support this and that a corpse that was dead of any complaint might fall into just such an attitude as this body has assumed.

With no clues to indicate in which period this individual lived or to suggest his identity, it is idle to speculate on the circumstances surrounding his death. It is reasonable to assume that he was of noble, if not Royal birth, or a member of the priesthood.

Height of the Body 1.709 metres.

The Coffin: Cairo Museum Catalogue Number **61023.**

Probably a replacement coffin used for this mummy. No inscription or any traces of previous inscription provide any clue to the identity of the mummy or the original owner of the coffin.

The coffin is made from cedar which has been painted white.

Length of the coffin 1.95 metres. Breadth 0.60 metres.
Height 0.56 metres.

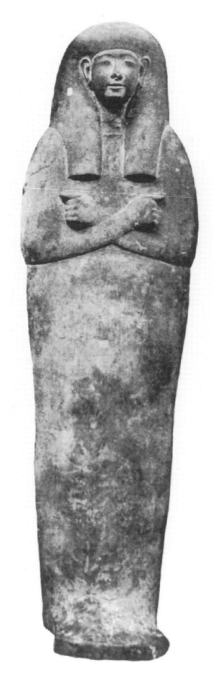

The lid of the coffin of an Unknown Man (Fig 127)

SETI I.   19th Dynasty.   1291-1278 B.C.

Son of the founder of the 19th Dynasty, Ramesses I, Seti did much to restore Egypt's military power. He was a prolific builder. His main surviving monuments include his great temple to the Gods at Abydos and his tomb in the Valley of the Kings (number 17) which is the largest ever excavated there.

The Mummy: Found in the Royal Cache at Deir el Bahri in 1881.
Cairo Museum Catalogue Number **61077**.
Exhibition Number **6350**.

The body of Seti I was unwrapped by Maspero in Cairo, on June 9th 1886.

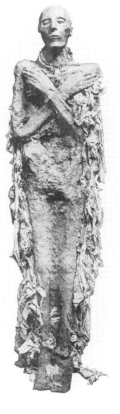

The mummy of Seti I (Fig 128)

The identification of the mummy was made by three separate hieratic inscriptions written on the coffin lid. These reveal that

151

before being laid to rest in the tomb at Deir el Bahri, the mummy of Seti I lay for a while in the tomb of Princess Anhapou and then the tomb of Amenhotep I.

The whole body is covered with a black mass of bandages, impregnated with resin. All the exposed areas of flesh, including the face, are now black, although Maspero clearly states that when the mummy was first exposed, the flesh was distinctly brown in colour.

The arms are crossed over the chest in the manner of the 18th Dynasty Kings, but the hands are open against the chest.

The left side of the chest is stuffed with a mass of resin-impregnated linen, now set solid. The heart remains within the body cavity, as was customary, but has been displaced by the embalmers and now lies on the right-hand side of the chest.

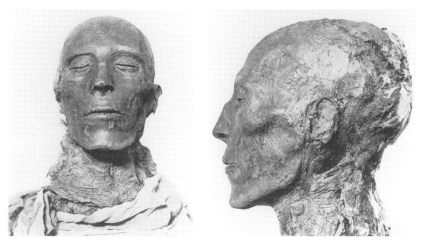

The head of the mummy of Seti I (Figs 129 and 130)

The head is in a remarkably good state of preservation, despite having been broken from the body by robbers. The head is shaven, the eyes closed. Seti exhibits markedly different features from the Kings of the 18th Dynasty, as is to be expected from a new ruling Dynasty.

X-Rays have revealed that the robbers missed a few beads and an 'Eye of Horus' amulet, which remained hidden in the resin-soaked bandages.

Neither Elliot Smith or the Michigan team were able to put a definite age to Seti when he died. He must have been into his middle age.

Height of the body, 1.665 metres.

The Coffin: Cairo Museum Catalogue Number **61019.**
              Exhibition Number **3881**

The coffin which contained the mummy of Seti I was probably part of the King's original burial equipment.

Made of cedar wood, originally it would have been overlaid with plaster and gilded. The priests of the 21st Dynasty, who restored the burial, found the coffin scraped of all the gold and the face irretrievably scarred. They arranged for the face to be re-modelled. It was reduced in size, leaving the original inlaid eyes of blue glass and white limestone, with black obsidian pupils, looking today strangely large, in the white painted face.

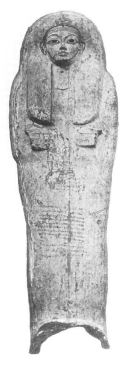

The lid of the coffin of Seti I (Fig 131)

Details of the ears and the chin line have been drawn in a hasty, but highly competent manner. Two cartouches were drawn at the same time upon the middle of the coffin, together with a long hieratic inscription recording the pious work of the re-burial commissions.

Length of the coffin 2.15 metres. Breadth 0.73 metres.
Height 0.68 metres.

153

Ramesses II.　　　　19th Dynasty.　　　　1279-1212 B.C.

Son of Seti I, Ramesses was a great soldier and led many campaigns against the enemies of Egypt. He too was a prolific builder, adding to existing temples and building new. His name appears throughout the country, for he frequently usurped the statues and buildings of earlier Pharaohs. His main monuments include the Ramesseum at Thebes and the temples of Abu Simbel in Nubia.

Ramesses had many wives and is reputed to have had over one hundred children. Original tomb in the Valley of the Kings number 7.

The Mummy:　Found in the Royal Cache at Deir el Bahri in 1881.
　　　　　　　Cairo Museum Catalogue Number **61078.**
　　　　　　　Exhibition Number **6351.**

The mummy of Ramesses II was unwrapped on June 1st 1886.

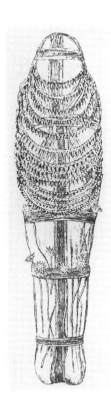

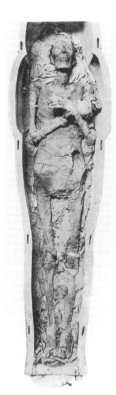

The wrapped mummy of Ramesses II, covered in floral garlands, placed on the mummy by the restorers of the burial.
(Fig 132)

This drawing was made by Schweinfurth soon after the discovery.

The mummy of Ramesses II
(Fig 133)

A note written in hieroglyphs identified the body and stated that in the tenth year of the priest Pinudjem (c.1060 B.C.), the mummy was moved to the tomb of Amenhotep I, at the same time as the mummy of Seti I.

Both X-Rays and a visual examination, show a considerable resemblance between Seti and Ramesses.

The mummy is well preserved, despite rough treatment at the hands of robbers, during which the genital organs have been broken off and lost.

The greater part of the body is still enclosed in resin-soaked linen bandages. The limbs are little more than skin clinging to the bones but the face is better preserved.

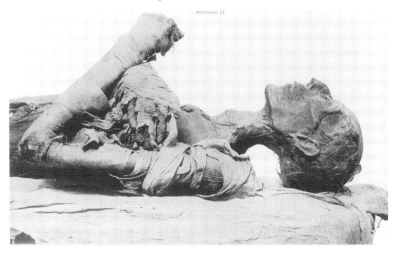

The mummy of Ramesses II (detail) (Fig 134)

The temples and back of the head are covered with fine silky hair, about 6 centimetres long, now yellow in colour. The recent examination of the mummy by the French showed that this colouring is probably natural, but were unable to identify a dilute yellow pigment which was discovered. If Ramesses did have naturally red hair this would have been a rare thing in a predominantly dark-haired race.

It is possible that the colouring of both the hair and the skin are as a result of the mummification process. The face was originally painted (probably red-ochre) and traces of darker paint remain around the eyebrows.

The nostrils have been carefully packed with resin and the mouth too appears to be full of a similar substance.

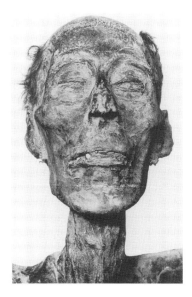

Some of the resin was removed from the mouth by Elliot Smith, revealing the front teeth. Elliot Smith stated that the teeth appeared to be good, but X-Rays have revealed that the King must have suffered severe dental problems during the latter years of his life.

Hair stubble can be seen on the upper lip and chin. The pores of the skin are large on the neck and blackheads are visible.

The ears have also been smeared with resin paste. The lobes have been pierced as was the fashion.

X-Rays have also revealed severe degenerative arthritis of the hip joint and arteriosclerosis of the lower legs, which would have caused poor circulation of the blood and made movement painful.

The age of the King at death was at least eighty years, possibly more.

Robins and Shute, who have studied X-Rays of the mummy and the proportions of the limbs, have revealed that the lower legs of Ramesses are short in relation to the rest of the body and that the "proportions are anomalous almost to the point of deformity". This feature is not obvious from a visual examination of the mummy. Over recent years, the state of preservation of the mummy caused concern. In 1976 the mummy was sent to the Musée de l'Homme in Paris, for conservation. The opportunity was taken for a complete examination of the body, using a variety of modern scientific techniques, although with the exception of some hair, no tissue samples were allowed to be taken from the body.

It was found that the main cause of the deterioration of the mummy was bacteria. The mummy was 'radiosterilised', using radio-active gamma rays. Some of the bandages on the body were cleaned and replaced.

The French also undertook the conservation of the shell of the King's coffin and made a special stretcher to support the mummy and facilitate easier handling of the body in the future.

Height of the body, 1.733 metres.

The Coffin: Cairo Museum Catalogue Number **61020.**
                  Exhibition Number **3877.**

The mummy of Ramesses II was found in a magnificent cedar wood coffin.

This coffin was probably selected by the priests of the 21st Dynasty as being the most suitable for Ramesses, whose original burial equipment must have been damaged beyond repair, or missing.

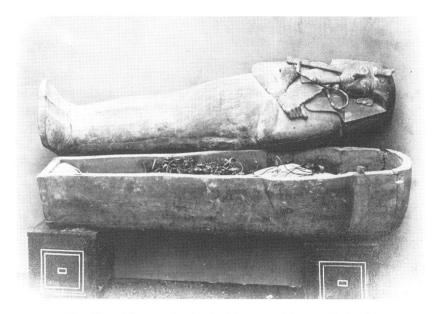

The coffin and the wrapped and garlanded mummy of Ramesses II (Fig 136)

The coffin has been dated, on stylistic grounds, to the end of the 18th Dynasty. It was undoubtedly made for a Royal burial. The original owner can only be one of three Pharaohs: Ay, Horemheb or

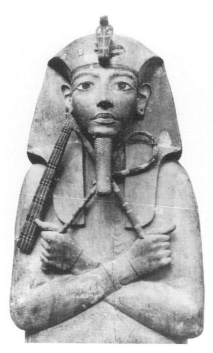

The lid of the coffin of Ramesses II (Fig 137)

possibly Ramesses I of the 19th Dynasty. The tombs of all three Kings have been discovered, but their mummies have not been found (unless they are included in some of the unidentified mummies from the Cache at Deir el Bahri and the tomb of Amenhotep II).

The original decoration of gold over a plaster coating, has now disappeared from the coffin. The wood is now bare, with traces of yellow paint on the wood and details in black lines of bracelets, necklaces and outlining the eyes.

The coffin is similar in style to those of Tutankhamun, and shows the King wearing the Nemset head-dress.

The cobra on the brow of the King and the Crook and Flail are of inferior workmanship and were undoubtedly added during the 21st Dynasty to replace the missing originals.

Two large, irregular cartouches have been written on the abdomen, giving the names of the King. An inscription written below the cartouches details the re-burial.

Length of the coffin, 2.06 metres. Breadth 0.545 metres. Height, 0.71 metres.

MERNEPTAH.   19th Dynasty.   1212-1202 B. C.

A son of Ramesses II and Queen Isinefre, Merneptah came to the throne following the death of the heir apparent, Prince Amenhirkopshef, son of Queen Nefertari. He continued the warrior tradition and successfully repelled an invasion of Egypt by the Libyans. Original tomb in the Valley of the Kings, number 8.

The Mummy: Found in the tomb of Amenhotep II in 1898.
    Cairo Museum Catalogue Number **61079**.
    Exhibition Number **6352**.

The mummy of Merneptah was unwrapped by Elliot Smith on July 8th 1907.

An inscription identified this mummy and the embalming techniques also date this mummy to the 19th Dynasty.

The body was wrapped in a fine sheet of linen which hid a hastily wrapped mummy and a mass of loose rags which were the remains of the original wrappings.

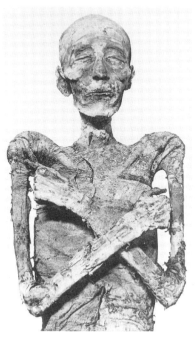

The mummy of Merneptah (detail) (Fig 138)

159

The mummy had been badly treated by robbers, who had driven a knife or axe through the shoulder, broken off the right forearm and hacked a hole through the abdomen.

The body is that of an old man who probably suffered badly from arthritis. Like Ramesses II there is evidence of arteriosclerosis.

X-Rays revealed signs of fractures in the heads of the femurs and there is a hole in the right side of the cranium, possibly made after death.

Merneptah was bald at death and probably corpulent. The nose has been flattened by the bandages but is similar to the noses of Ramesses II and Seti I. The nostrils have been plugged with resin. Traces of paint survive on the eyebrows and the King's ears have been pierced.

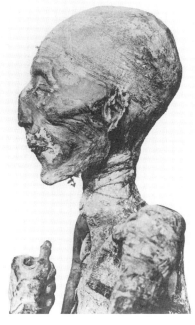

The head of the mummy of Merneptah (Fig 139)

The hands are clenched and may have originally held the symbols of Royalty.

The body is covered by an encrustation of sodium chloride; the results of the embalming. The body cavity has been filled with a white 'cheesy' material, probably decomposed butter and soda.

There is one curious feature, in that the scrotum of the King is missing and the exposed flesh has been covered with a layer of resin.

160

This shows that he must have been castrated either shortly before his death (which is unlikely) or during the embalming process, for reasons unknown.

The King had poor teeth and some were lost before his death. Several dentists have wondered if these teeth were deliberately removed, rather than just falling out. If this was so, it would be rare evidence of dental surgery to survive from Ancient Egypt.

Height of the body, 1.714 metres.

The Coffin: Cairo Museum Catalogue Number **61039.**

The base of this coffin contained the mummy of Merneptah, whilst the down turned lid contained the mummy of an unknown woman.

For the description of this coffin and illustration, see page 166/167.

SETI II.   19th Dynasty.   1199-1193 B.C.

Seti II was the son of Merneptah, and his chief wife was Queen Tausret. He built a small temple in the forecourt of the temple of Karnak.

Original tomb in the Valley of the Kings, number **15.**

The Mummy: Found in the tomb of Amenhotep II in 1898.
                Cairo Museum Catalogue Number **61081.**
                Exhibition Number **6354.**

The mummy of Seti II was unwrapped by Elliot Smith on September 3rd 1905.

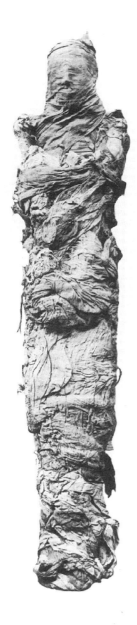

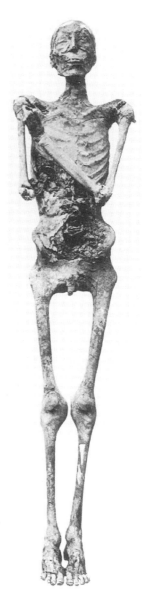

The wrapped mummy of Seti II (Fig 140)

Bundles of linen, which proved to be shirts, were included in the wrappings of the mummy.

The mummy of Seti II (Fig 141)

The body had been carefully mummified and was wrapped in exceptionally fine linen. Thick layers of resinous paste cover the body and bandages. In some areas the fingerprints of the embalmers can be seen. The body cavity has been packed with resin soaked bandages, which have set solid.

The head of the mummy has been broken off by robbers.

The arms too have been broken, with the right forearm missing. Originally the arms would have been folded against the chest.

The head, and particularly the face, is covered in resinous paste. The King's hair has been cropped short. The ears are pierced.

The teeth are in a surprisingly good condition, except for some slight wear.

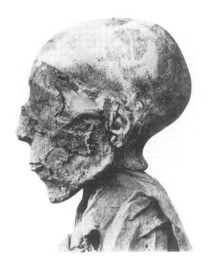

The head of the mummy of Seti II (Fig 142)

Seti was probably in his thirties when he died.

The robbers missed a few beads and scarabs which still remained in the wrappings. Fragments of several garments and two perfectly preserved shirts were also found included in the wrappings of the mummy. Some of the material was a particularly fine muslin, many pieces with elaborately fringed and coloured (red and blue) borders.

Elliot Smith pointed out that the features of Seti are very different from the other 19th Dynasty Pharaohs, but that they do recall in a striking manner those of the 18th Dynasty. His small, narrow and high-bridged nose is not unlike that of Amenhotep II and Thutmose IV. Even the method of embalming is similar to the 18th Dynasty. The identity of this mummy must, therefore, be suspect. It is possible that this may be an 18th Dynasty Pharaoh, possibly Thutmose I or II, as the identification of the mummies of these Pharaohs is by no means certain.

Height of the body, 1.640 metres.

The Coffin: Cairo Museum Catalogue Number **61037.**

The mummy of Seti II was found in a lidless wooden coffin. This coffin had been re-used, but the name of the original owner is not known.

The names of Seti have been added by the restorers of the burial.

Length of the coffin 1.85 metres. Breadth 0.43 metres. Height 0.27 metres.

Note: This coffin is not illustrated.

UNKNOWN WOMAN.   19th Dynasty.   Date uncertain.

The Mummy: Found in the Tomb of Amenhotep II in 1898.
                 Cairo Museum Catalogue Number **61082.**

This wrapped mummy was found in the down-turned lid of the coffin of Setnakht.

At the sole of each foot was a large bundle wrapped in coarse cloth and fixed in position by the bandages of the right leg.

The parcel on the right foot contained a mass of epidermis mixed with large quantities of natron. The parcel on the left contained portions of the viscera also mixed with natron.

After removing the head bandages, some of which had been wound in a circular manner, with others in a figure of eight, the hair was found to be enclosed in a piece of linen the size of a man's handkerchief. It was placed on the head and the lateral corners brought round to the forehead and tied in a knot.

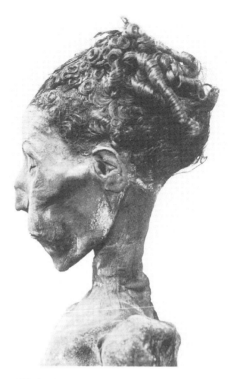

The head of the mummy of an Unknown Woman (Fig 144)

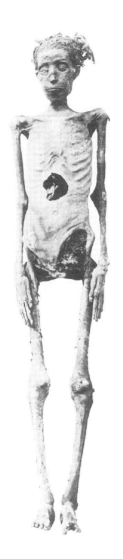

The mummy of an Unknown Woman (Fig 143)

The hair is well preserved in a series of sharply rolled curls.

The woman has a prominent, narrow and high-bridged nose which has been flattened by the pressure of the bandages.

The packing of the mouth has given the face a pouting expression.

The arms are placed vertically at the side of the body with the hands resting on the thighs.

This mummy has escaped serious damage from tomb robbers except for a large rounded hole made through the brittle anterior abdominal wall.

The embalming techniques used indicate that the body was not embalmed before the latter part of the 19th Dynasty. Her association, in the tomb of Amenhotep II, with the mummies of late 19th and early 20th Dynasty Kings, could indicate that this unknown woman was of the Royal family. A tentative identification could be Tausret, Queen of Siptah and Seti II.

Height of the body 1.589 metres.

The Coffin: Cairo Museum Catalogue Number **61039.**

This coffin is probably one of the original coffins made for Setnakht (c. 1185-1182 B.C.). Made of cartonnage, it has been badly treated at the hands of robbers.

The coffin lid and base had become separated in the Tomb of Amenhotep II.

The base enclosed the mummy of Merneptah, whilst the down-turned lid contained an unidentified female mummy.

The cartonnage is made of five or six layers of material, stuck together and covered in a layer of plaster over which was stuck another layer of material.

The coffin base is made of cartonnage 'planks' laced together with leather thongs.

The feet of the lid had been made separately and are now missing from the coffin.

The whole coffin is covered in a red-brown varnish showing traces of a 'rishi' design painted in white on a black background. Parts of the coffin must have once been gilded, for they have been adzed over.

Broken fragments of the coffin and feet were found elsewhere in the tomb.

Length of the coffin 1.87 metres. Breadth 0.48 metres.
Height 0.50 metres.

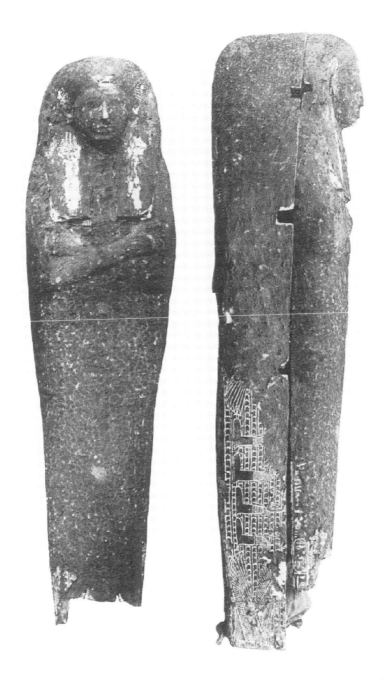

The coffin of Setnakht (Fig 145)

SIPTAH.   19th Dynasty.   1193-1187 B.C.

Son of Seti II, Siptah probably came to the throne by marrying Queen Tausret. Original tomb in the Valley of the Kings, number 47.

The Mummy: Found in the tomb of Amenhotep II in 1898.
Cairo Museum Catalogue Number **61080**.
Exhibition Number **6353**.

The unwrapping of the mummy of Siptah by Elliot Smith was started on August 29th 1905 and took three days to complete. All the original bandages had been smeared with paste; some still bore the imprints of the long stolen jewellery.

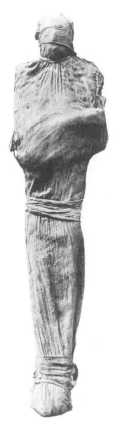

The wrapped mummy of Siptah (Fig 146)

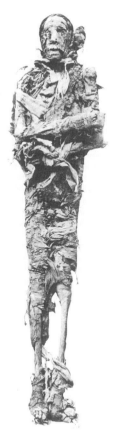

The mummy of Siptah (Fig 147)

The body is that of a man who probably died in his late teens or early twenties.

The right forearm was broken by robbers and the priests of the 21st Dynasty used wooden splints to restore the mummy.

The face was completely covered with a mass of black resin, some of which Elliot Smith was able to remove. The cheeks are packed with fine muslin. Lichen was used to pack the body cavity.

A thick crop of red-brown curly hair remains on the head.

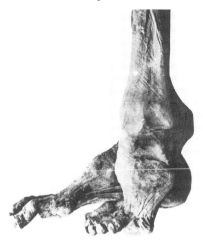

The feet of the mummy of Siptah (Fig 148)

The mummy is particularly interesting from the medical point of view, because of a severe deformity of the left foot. It was originally diagnosed as being a club foot, but the Michigan team were able to show from their study that the overall shortening of the entire right leg and the deformed foot indicates the presence of a neuro-muscular disease in childhood. One disorder which produces these symptoms, is poliomyelitis. Polio has only been identified once before in Dynastic Egypt and then only tentatively from a relief carving. This possible diagnosis was one of the major findings of the Michigan team.

Height of the body 1.638 metres.

The Coffin: Cairo Museum Catalogue Number **61038.**

The mummy of Siptah was found in a wooden coffin, probably of sycamore, which has been dated to the 19th Dynasty.

Once again it is a non-Royal coffin which has been used. The original owner may well have been female.

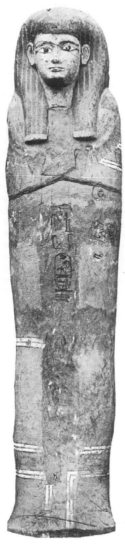

The coffin has been damaged by robbers. Parts of the surface have been attacked with a small adze-type tool, which indicates that these areas were probably covered originally with gold. The damage must have occurred before the re-burial, for the priests wrote the names and titles of the King in black paint, directly over the damaged parts.

Length of the coffin, 1.90 metres. Breadth 0.49 metres. Height 0.46 metres.

RAMESSES III.　　　　20th Dynasty.　　　　1182-1151 B.C.

When Ramesses III came to the throne, Egypt had been through a period of decline. Ramesses re-established the army and the navy. It was during his reign that one of the first recorded sea battles was fought.

His main surviving monument is his funerary temple at Medinet Habu. Original tomb in the Valley of the Kings, number 11.

The Mummy:　Found in the Royal Cache at Deir el Bahri in 1881.
　　　　　　　Cairo Museum Catalogue Number **61083.**
　　　　　　　Exhibition Number **6355.**

The mummy of Ramesses III is that of an old man; he was probably about sixty-five at the time of his death.

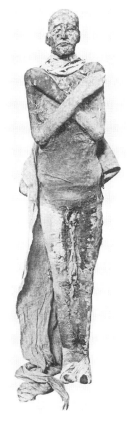

The mummy of Ramesses III
(Fig 150)

171

The body is still well wrapped, although most of the remaining bandages are those used by the restorers of the Royal burials in the 21st Dynasty.

The X-Rays of the mummy revealed statuettes of the four sons of Horus on the left side of the chest. The X-Rays, taken from two angles, pin-point exactly the location of these objects, but it is unlikely that they will ever be removed as such an operation might damage the body.

The arms of the King are folded over the chest, but like Seti I, the hands are open. At the time of Seti I this was an unusual occurrence, but after the reign of Ramesses III it is common.

The head is well preserved, although the nose has been flattened by the pressure of the bandages.

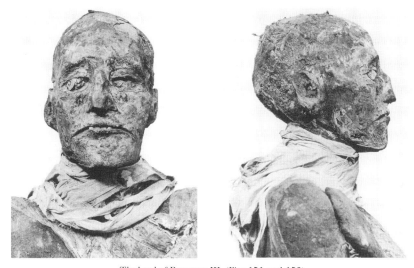

The head of Ramesses III (Figs 151 and 152)

Artificial eyes have been inserted into the eye sockets.

Dentally, Ramesses III bears a strong resemblance to Seti I and the other Kings of the 19th Dynasty.

It is often stated that the mummy of Ramesses III has been the model for 'The Mummy' in countless horror films.

Height of the body 1.683 metres.

The Coffin: Cairo Museum Catalogue Number 61021.

The mummy, enclosed in a rough coffin of cartonnage, was found in the coffin of Queen Ahmose-Nefertari of the 18th Dynasty. This enormous coffin was large enough to hold both the mummy of Ramesses III and the Queen.

The coffin of Ramesses III is of crude workmanship and the original gold overlay has been stripped by the robbers. The names and titles of the King have been painted on the front of the coffin.

Length of the coffin, 1.89 metres. Breadth 0.52 metres.
Height. 0.36 metres.

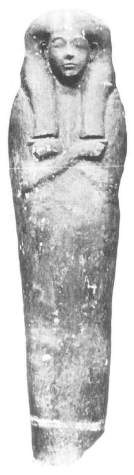

The lid of the coffin of Ramesses III (Fig 153)

A good illustration of the confusion faced by the priests restoring the Royal burials, is that in the tomb of Amenhotep II another damaged coffin base was found which bore the name of Ramesses III (Number 61040). This held the mummy of Amenhotep III.

RAMESSES IV. 20th Dynasty. 1151-1145 B.C.

Son of Ramesses III, Ramesses IV had a short, peaceful reign.
Original tomb in the Valley of the Kings, number 2.

The Mummy: Found in the tomb of Amenhotep II in 1898.
Cairo Museum Catalogue Number **61084.**
Exhibition Number **6356.**

The mummy of Ramesses IV was unwrapped by Elliot Smith on June 24th 1905. The body had been badly re-wrapped; a mass of rags had been thrown around the body and were held in place by a few tighter bandages. The mummy was covered by a shroud, on which was written the name of the King.

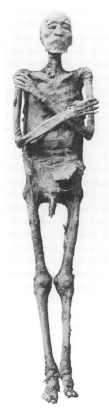

The mummy of Ramesses IV
(Fig 154)

The mummy is fairly well preserved; some of the original bandages still remain close to the skin.

The King is clean shaven and was quite bald at death. Traces of dark paint remain on the eyebrows. Onions were used to pack the eyes and the nostrils have been plugged with resin.

The mouth has been filled with paste, which still covers the lips. Some teeth are just visible and appear to be healthy, if worn. X-Rays confirm that Ramesses IV had better teeth than many of his predecessors.

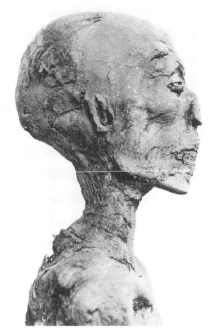

The head of the mummy of Ramesses IV (Fig 155)

The age of the King when he died is not known.

The arms are crossed over the body, with the hands open. The finger nails have been lost, either during the embalming process or the re-burial.

The body cavity has been filled with lichen (parmelia furfuracea) which was used only for Siptah and Ramesses IV.

The penis and scrotum still survive and have been bandaged separately, their lengths being 9.1 and 7.6 centimetres respectively.

The King seems to have been circumcised. A resin paste plug has been placed over the anus.

Height of the body, 1.604 metres.

The Coffin: Cairo Museum Catalogue Number **61041.**

The mummy of Ramesses IV was found in a poor coffin which has been dated to the 20th Dynasty.

Made of white-painted wood, the coffin is plain, except for a black painted inscription giving the names and titles of the King.

The coffin has arms crossed over the body and the hands hold the symbols of Osiris and Isis.

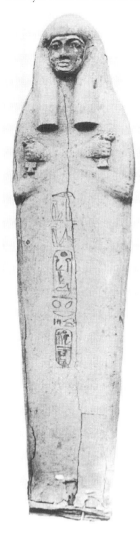

The lid of the coffin of Ramesses IV
(Fig 156)

Length of the coffin, 1.76 metres. Breadth 0.48 metres.
Height 0.34 metres.

RAMESSES V.   20th Dynasty.   1145-1141 B.C.

Ramesses V is thought to have been a usurper to the throne. He may have been the brother of Ramesses IV, but he was not the next in line.

He was himself deposed by the rightful heir, Ramesses VI, who also usurped his tomb in the Valley of the Kings (number 9).

The Mummy: Found in the tomb of Amenhotep II in 1898.
Cairo Museum Catalogue Number **61085.**
Exhibition Number **6357.**

The mummy of Ramesses V was unwrapped by Elliot Smith on June 25th 1905.

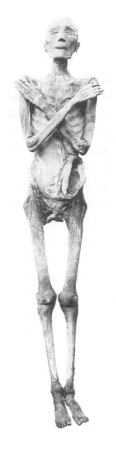

The mummy of Ramesses V
(Fig 157)

The body is well preserved, with little damage caused by the robbers who stripped the original wrappings from the body. The wrappings which have survived show evidence of the use of a sharp-bladed instrument to cut them from the body.

The face has been painted a red ochre colour. The cranial cavity and eye sockets have been packed with fine linen, the nostrils and mouth with wax.

The scalp is covered with short dark hair. During his life the King must have worn heavy ear-rings, for his pierced lobes have become greatly stretched.

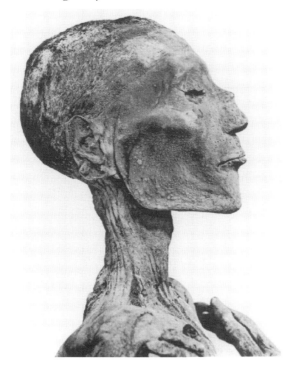

The head of the mummy
of Ramesses V (Fig 158)

The skin of the King is covered with small nodules. Elliot Smith proposed that they were evidence of smallpox. The Michigan team have been able to come up with no better explanation. Only a more detailed scientific examination of the tissues will confirm this theory.

The scrotum of the King remains; large and baggy, it has been flattened against the body by the bandages.

The abdomen has been packed with sawdust. The incision into the body is large and parts of the viscera have been left in the body by the embalmers .

There is a small hole in the skull which has been made *post mortem*, by the robbers, possibly to let out the 'evil spirits'. Similar holes appear in the skulls of the mummies of Merneptah, Seti II, Ramesses IV and Ramesses VI. All these mummies were found in the tomb of Amenhotep II.

The age of the King at death is uncertain.

Height of the body, 1.726 metres.

The Coffin: Cairo Museum Catalogue Number **61042.**

The mummy of Ramesses V was found in a plain white-painted, rectangular wooden coffin of the 18th Dynasty.

Length of the coffin, 1.77 metres. Breadth 0.41 metres.

Note: This coffin is not illustrated.

RAMESSES VI.   20th Dynasty.   1141-1133 B.C.

Ramesses VI was another son of Ramesses III whose mother was Queen Isis. By this time the Royal residence was established in the Delta, but the burials were still made at Thebes. Ramesses VI has a magnificent tomb in the Valley of the Kings (number 9) which was usurped from Ramesses V.

The Mummy: Found in the tomb of Amenhotep II in 1898.
                 Cairo Museum Catalogue Number **61086.**
                 Exhibition Number **6358.**

The mummy of Ramesses VI was unwrapped in Cairo on 8th July 1905. The body when revealed proved to be one of the worst damaged by tomb robbers. The head and the trunk have literally been hacked to pieces. The priests restoring the burial tied the fragments of the body to a board (from a coffin belonging to Setnakht) to restore some semblance of the usual shape of a mummy.

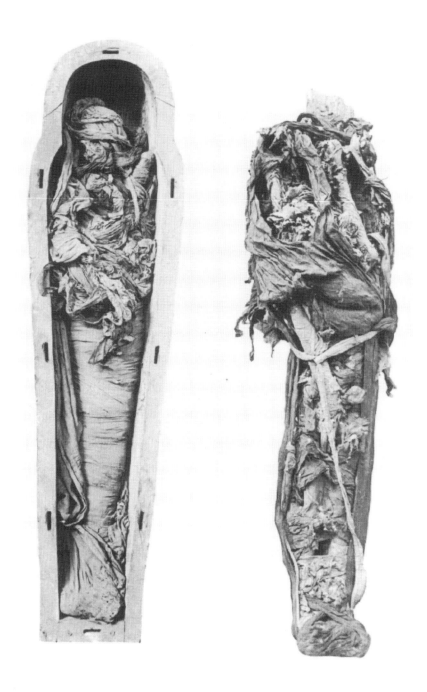

Two views of the partially unwrapped mummy of Ramesses VI (Fig 159)

The wrappings too were in a great state of disorder and included in them were some broken pieces of the head, the right hand of a woman and the mutilated right hand and forearm of another man.

Axe and knife cuts mark the head (all made after death). The right hand of the mummy is missing.

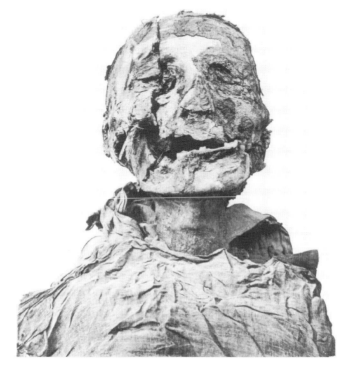

The head of the mummy of Ramesses VI (Fig 160)

The King was probably middle aged when he died. Elliot Smith was able to re-assemble the head from the fragments. It was originally thickly coated with resinous paste. The ears are pierced and the King's teeth are only slightly worn.

The Coffin: Cairo Museum Catalogue Number **61043.**

Made of sycamore, the anthropoid coffin used for Ramesses VI was originally made for a priest from the reign of Thutmose III of the 18th Dynasty.

The face has been broken away by robbers. It was originally painted yellow. The collar and bracelets of the coffin are painted blue, green and red. The rest of the coffin is black with the inscription picked out in yellow.

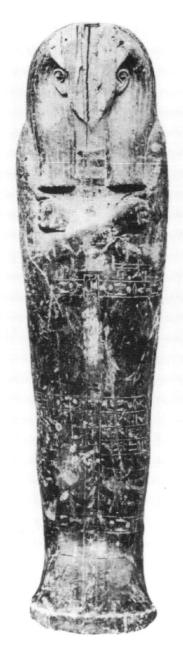

The lid of the coffin of Ramesses VI (Fig 161)

Length of the coffin 1.98 metres. Breadth 0.55.metres. Height 0.60 metres.

QUEEN NODJMET. 20th Dynasty. c. 1075 B.C.

Queen Nodjmet was the wife of the High Priest and King Herihor who ruled from Thebes at the end of the 20th Dynasty.

The Mummy: Found in the Royal Cache at Deir el Bahri in 1881.
Cairo Museum Catalogue Number **61087.**
Exhibition Number 6363.

The mummy of Queen Nodjmet has been disturbed by robbers in modern times and at least one item, a papyrus, was stolen. When unwrapped, more ancient damage to the mummy was revealed. Both wrists are broken and the left humerus and the legs are badly damaged.

The face has been cut by a sharp implement, presumably when the robbers were cutting their way through the bandages. Both cheeks and the forehead bear cuts. Similar wounds appear on the chest of the mummy.

A packing of sawdust and resin has been stuffed into the mouth to fill out the cheeks; as a result the face has taken on an almost circular shape.

Resin-coated bandages have been applied to the abdomen, legs, buttocks and other parts of the body to restore some of the original shape.

The embalming wound is plugged with a lump of wax.

The hands of the mummy are placed vertically alongside the hips, a position which was to become common from this time onwards.

The long dark hair is arranged in tight plaits, supplemented with additional plaits of false hair.

Unusually, the eyebrows are emphasised by the addition of whisps of human hair gummed into position.

Artificial eyes made of black and white stone have been inserted into the eye sockets. This is the earliest attempt known to represent the pupils of the eyes.

X-Rays have revealed that the Queen suffered from bad dentition, a problem with virtually all of the Royal mummies. Also revealed were fragments of jewellery missed by the robbers and the Queen's heart scarab and figures of the Four Sons of Horus placed within the body cavity with the embalmed viscera.

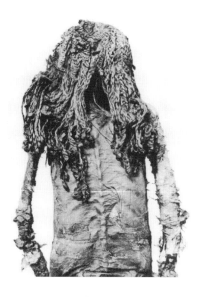

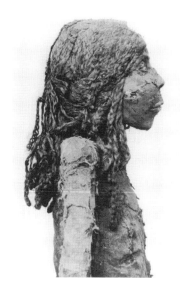

The mummy of Queen Nodjmet (detail)
(Figs 162, 163 and 164)

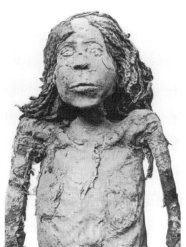

From this period the internal organs were removed from the body to be preserved, after which they were wrapped and returned to the body.

The embalming technique used for this mummy differs radically from that used previously and shows the transformation to the methods perfected in the next Dynasty.

The age of the Queen at death is estimated at between thirty and thirty-five.

Height of the Body 1.548 metres.

184

The Coffins: Cairo Museum Catalogue Number **61024.**

The Queen was found within two coffins, both of which were probably originally made for a male burial, appropriated and altered for her use. Both are made of cedar wood with a sycamore face.

The First Coffin: **61024A.** Exhibition Number **3858.**

This coffin has been badly damaged at the hands of robbers. All the once-gilded surfaces have been adzed over. Virtually none of the original inlaid decoration remain and the inlaid eyes have been lost.

The head-dress is painted blue.

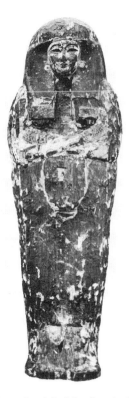

The lid of the first coffin of Queen Nodjmet (Fig 165)

The interior of the coffin lid is painted with black pitch and has no funerary scenes or inscriptions. The interior of the base is painted a red-brown colour, with funerary scenes drawn in white.

Length of the coffin 2.08 metres. Breadth 0.73 metres.
Height 0.80 metres.

The Second Coffin: 61024B.

Like the first coffin, the second has been badly damaged by the robbers. The greater proportion of the once-gilded areas have been adzed over, but on this coffin the sacred images are untouched, with gilding and coloured inlay remaining.

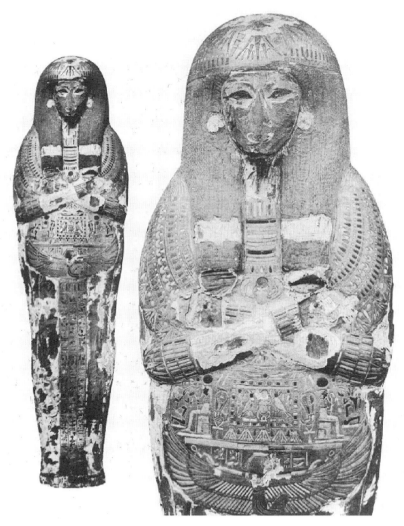

The lid of the second coffin of Queen Nodjmet (Fig 166)

The hands of the coffin and the inlaid eyes are missing.

The interior of the coffin is decorated with finely painted funerary scenes.

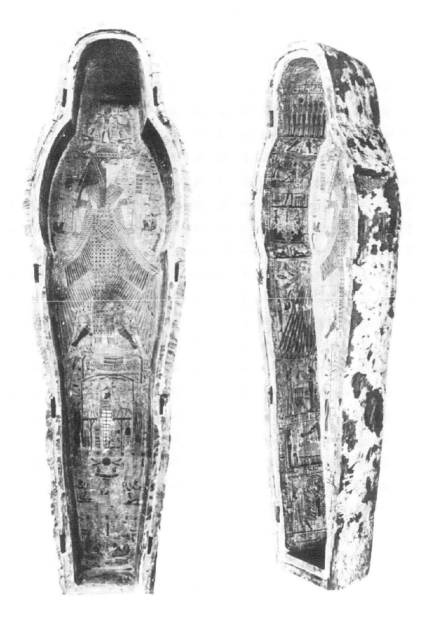

The base of the second coffin of Queen Nodjmet, showing the interior decoration (Fig 167)

Length of the coffin 1.88 metres. Breadth 0.58 metres.
Height 0.57 metres.

THE 21ST AND 22ND DYNASTIES   c. 1069-525 B.C.

At some point during the reign of Ramesses XI (c. 1098-1070 B.C.) a military man called Herihor assumed the position of High Priest of Amun at Thebes. From the year 19 of Ramesses, Herihor styled himself King in the area around Thebes. He was portrayed on reliefs as Pharaoh, even though Ramesses was still alive and ruling from the North. Herihor retained his position as High Priest.

The burials of the 'High Priest Kings' were made at Thebes and although the trappings of Royalty are shown on reliefs and on papyri, their burials lack many of the expected 'Royal' features. The coffins, for example, are essentially the same as those of high-ranking commoners.

The Royal Tombs at Tanis, although slightly later, all retain the features of earlier Royal Burials and include considerable amounts of gold and silver.

The Theban burials are poor by comparison. Perhaps because of this, many of the later mummies were substantially intact when discovered.

Much can be made of this; it could mean that the greater proportion of the wealth of the country was centred around Tanis in the North, with Thebes being the 'poor relation'.

It could also mean that the Priest Kings of Thebes had realised that the sheer wealth buried with the bodies of earlier Kings virtually invited their destruction at the hands of tomb robbers and that they were content to enter their afterlife with less substantial funerary goods.

It was during these Dynasties that many of the New Kingdom Royal burials were restored following robberies. As a final desperate measure, the surviving Royal remains were collected together in the tomb of Amenhotep II in the Valley of the Kings and at a remote tomb at Deir el Bahri (known to us as Tomb DB 320). This particular tomb must have been considered 'safe' and was also used for the burials of some of the Priest-Kings and members of their families.

It is possible that the close contact with the royal remains of previous Dynasties revealed the inadequacies of the mummification treatment they had received. The mummification methods used from this period on improved dramatically. Great efforts were made to restore a more life-like appearance to the mummies.

It is interesting to note that, probably at the same time as the Theban Priest-Kings were arranging for the re-burial of the Royal mummies, the Royal tombs and the remains of their burials were being systematically and deliberately dismantled. Any remaining items were taken away to be recycled. Many of these objects found their way to the Northern city of Tanis and were incorporated in the Royal burials there, not in the 'Royal' burials at Thebes.

QUEEN DUATHATHOR-HENTTAWY. 21st Dynasty. c. 1050 B.C.

Duathathor-Henttawy was the Queen of Pinudjem I.

The Mummy: Found in the Royal Cache at Deir el Bahri in 1881.
Cairo Museum Catalogue Number 61090.
Exhibition Number 6365.

The mummy of Duathathor-Henttawy was unwrapped by Maspero in 1881. The wrapped body had been disturbed by robbers who had dug through the layers of bandages over the throat and abdomen.

This mummy was given very elaborate treatment by the embalmers in an attempt to restore the form of the body and a life-like appearance.

Every part of the body has been packed internally to restore the shape of the limbs.

The neck is packed with a quantity of a fatty substance (probably butter and soda) to fill out the skin to give it the plump appearance of a living person, in contrast to the shrunken and emaciated necks of earlier mummies. The packing was introduced through the embalming incision in the abdomen.

The body cavity is filled with sawdust, forced between the skin and the underlying muscular tissue. The breasts have been moulded in linen.

The legs and arms are also packed. This was done from the body cavity as far as possible, but additional incisions were made in the skin of the knees, feet and shoulders.

The embalmers were not, however, successful with this technique as the body has been over-packed. An exceptionally large quantity of packing was introduced into the mouth, which has stretched the skin and caused the cheeks to burst.

The Queen's natural hair has been supplemented with artificial plaited strands which now completely frame the face. The skin of the face is painted yellow with the cheeks and lips highlighted in red and the eyebrows detailed in black.

Although the body has been ransacked by robbers, a gold plate remained covering the embalming incision.

The internal organs have been preserved separately and replaced in the body cavity.

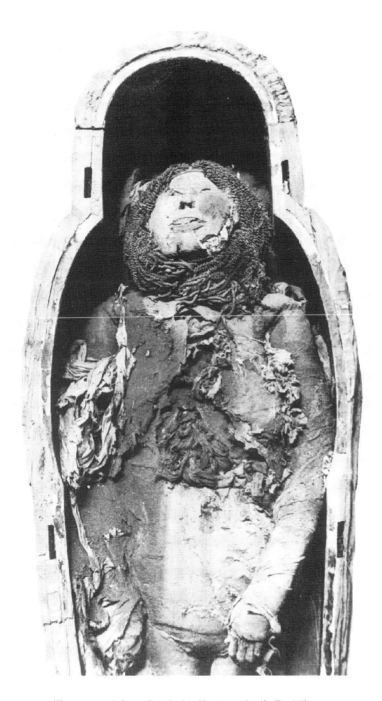

The mummy of Queen Duathathor-Henttawy (detail) (Fig 168)

X-Rays indicate an age at death of between thirty and forty and also revealed several small amulets remaining in the wrappings.

In life the Queen was probably quite plump.

The mummy of the Queen has recently been restored by Dr. Iskander of the Cairo Museum. The restoration has completely transformed the appearance of this mummy. The face has been re-attached to the head, and no longer looks as if it has burst. The yellow ochre paint on the face has been re-touched with a fine layer of wax.

The solidified salts and packing of the body cavity have been removed.

The gold plate which covered the embalming incision has been detached from the body. It is currently on separate display in the Cairo Museum.

Height of the body 1.518 metres.

The Coffins: Cairo Museum Catalogue Number **61026.**

The two coffins of Duathathor-Henttawy resemble the coffins of Queen Nodjmet and Pinudjem and probably were made in the same period.

Both are replacement coffins used by the restorers of the burial.

The First Coffin: **61026A.**

Only the base of the first coffin survives, in a damaged state. Most of the original gilded decoration has been adzed away both on the outside and inside of the box which is painted blue. The images of the Gods remain on the exterior whilst the bands of inscriptions have been removed.

Length of the coffin 2.15 metres. Breadth 0.71 metres.
Height 0.49 metres.

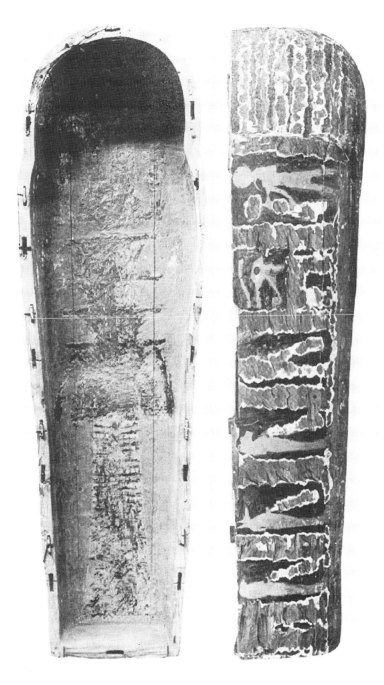

The base of the first coffin of Queen Duathathor-Henttawy (Fig 169)

The Second Coffin: 61026B.

The Second coffin too has been badly damaged. The lid survives but virtually all the gilded decoration has been removed. The hands and inlaid eyes have been lost.

Gilded winged Goddesses and a vertical band of inscriptions survive on the coffin lid.

The wig is painted blue.

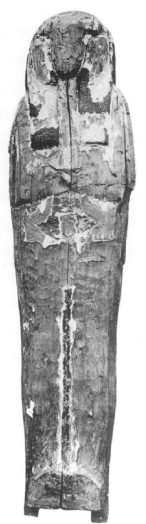

The lid of the second coffin of Queen Duathathor-Henttawy (Fig 170)

Length of the coffin 2.01 metres. Breadth 0.55 metres. Height 0.46 metres.

MAATKARE-MUTEMHET.   21st Dynasty.   c. 1020 B.C.

Maatkare-Mutemhet was a daughter of Queen Duathathor-Henttawy and Pinudjem I.

The Mummy: Found in the Royal Cache at Deir el Bahri in 1881.
Cairo Museum Catalogue Number 61088.
Exhibition Number 6364.

The mummy of Maatkare-Mutemhet was treated in a similar manner to the mummy of her mother Duathathor-Henttawy. It was unwrapped by Elliot Smith in June 1909.

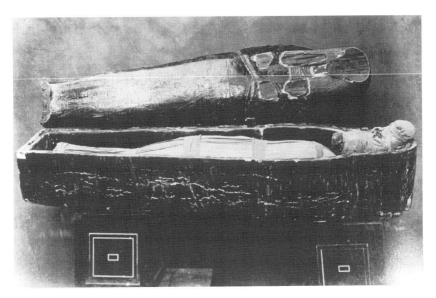

The inner coffin and wrapped mummy of Queen Maatkare-Mutemhet
showing the small mummy at the head, presumed to be that of her baby (Fig 171)

Despite damage by robbers, it is still possible to see that all parts of the body have been packed to restore their shape.

The body was wrapped in extremely fine linen. A coat of yellow ochre paint and gum over the body has caused the linen to adhere to the skin.

The breasts are moulded in linen. The real breasts were enormously enlarged at death. From this, and the evidence of a small mummy placed in the same coffin, Elliot Smith assumed that

Maatkare-Mutemhet had died in childbirth. The packing of the body cavity also indicated that she had given birth just before death.

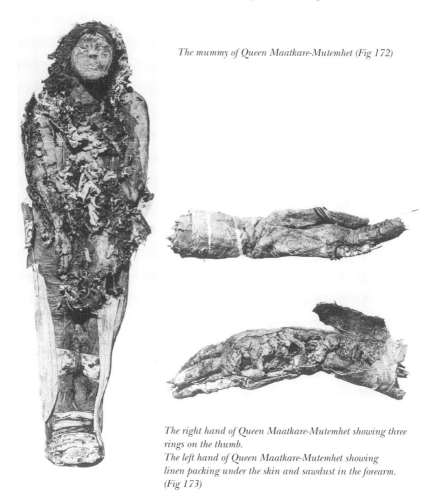

The mummy of Queen Maatkare-Mutemhet (Fig 172)

The right hand of Queen Maatkare-Mutemhet showing three rings on the thumb.
The left hand of Queen Maatkare-Mutemhet showing linen packing under the skin and sawdust in the forearm. (Fig 173)

X-Rays provided the first glimpse beneath the bandages of the small mummy, which Elliot Smith did not unwrap. This revealed that it was not in fact the body of a baby, but of a female hamadryas baboon. The fate of the child is unknown, as are the reasons for the inclusion of the animal mummy which has been (and probably will remain) a matter of great speculation.

Maatkare-Mutemhet's ear lobes are pierced and have become stretched from the wearing of heavy ear-rings. The dark brown hair shows some traces of grey.

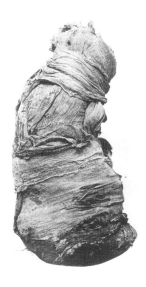

The wrapped mummy initially thought to be that of the child of Matkare-Mutemhet, but now known to be that of a baboon (Fig 174)

A leather thong is tied around the head to support an amulet (now missing). Three gold and silver rings remain on the hands. These rings can be seen in illustration on the previous page which also shows the packing of the limbs to restore a life-like appearance.

Height of the body 1.522 metres.

The Coffins: Cairo Museum Catalogue Number **61028.**

The Mummy of Maatkare-Mutemhet was found enclosed within two coffins, which were probably those actually made for her.

The mummy, which was enclosed in the second coffin was covered by a 'coffin board'. Resembling the lids of the coffins, these boards have no coffin box and are only a few centimetres thick. The coffin board lay directly on the mummy and was included as a part of the funerary equipment for burials from the 18th Dynasty onwards. Many survive from non-Royal burials and only feature as part of Royal burials from the 21st Dynasty onwards.

The First Coffin: 61028A. Exhibition Number 3852.

Made of cedar and acacia wood, this coffin is exceptionally well preserved and virtually undamaged by robbers. The gilded right hand is missing. In the forehead remain holes which once held the head of the Vulture head-dress covering the large wig.

The coffin is heavily gilded and covered in superbly painted funerary texts and sacred images.

Length of the coffin 2.23 metres. Breadth 0.77 metres. Height 0.56 metres.

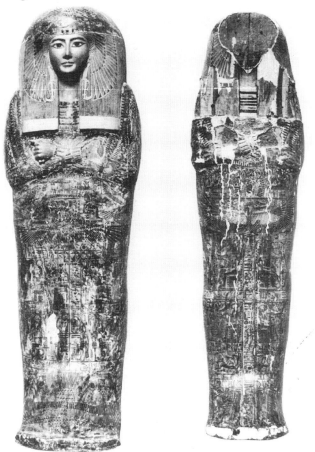

The lids of the first and second coffins of Queen Maatkare-Mutemhet (Fig 175)

The Second Coffin: 61028B.

Similar in design and decoration to the first coffin, this smaller version has been badly damaged by robbers who have removed both the gilded hands and the face.

Length of the coffin 1.96 metres. Breadth 0.57 metres. Height 0.66 metres.

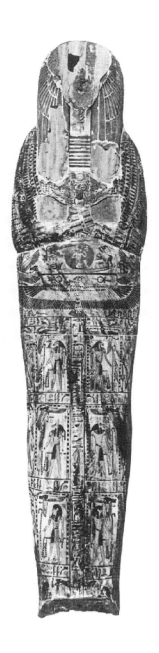

The coffin board of Queen Maatkare-Mutemhet (Fig 176)

The Coffin Board: 61028C.

Placed directly over the wrapped mummy, this board is also similar in design to the two coffins.

    Once again robbers have removed the gilded hands and face.

Length of the board 1.81 metres. Breadth 0.46 metres.

MASAHARTA.   21st Dynasty.   c. 1055-1046 B.C.

Masaharta was a General and High Priest of Amun at Thebes.

The Mummy: Found in the Royal Cache at Deir el Bahri in 1881.
Cairo Museum Catalogue Number **61092**.

The mummy of Masaharta has received the same treatment as the Queens of this period.

The face has been over-packed and is painted with red ochre. The whole body is covered with a coating of red ochre and gum.

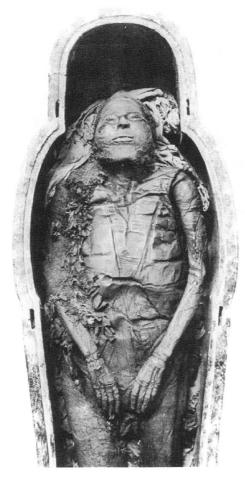

The mummy of Masaharta (detail) (Fig 177)

The hands are placed over the pubic region, but do not reach because of the great corpulence of the packed mummy.

It is likely that Masaharta was corpulent when he died. The body is intact. The skin shows clearly the indentations made by the first layer of bandages, which were impregnated with resin. Impressions of (now lost) jewellery also remain on the skin.

One gold finger stall remains on the middle finger of the right hand.

Height of the body 1.696 metres.

The Coffins: Cairo Museum Catalogue Number **61027.**

Masaharta was buried in a set of cedar coffins made for him. The two coffins and the coffin board are identical in design.

The first coffin (**61027A**) is substantially intact, with one gilded hand missing.

The face is gilded and is framed by a large wig painted in blue and yellow stripes.

The second coffin (**61027B**) and coffin board (**61027C**) have both lost their hands and faces. Both coffins and board are covered in finely painted funerary scenes.

The first coffin: Length 2.18 metres. Breadth 0.80 metres. Height 1.04 metres.

The second coffin: Length 2.0 metres. Breadth 0.60 metres. Height 0.69 metres.

(No measurements are available for the coffin board).

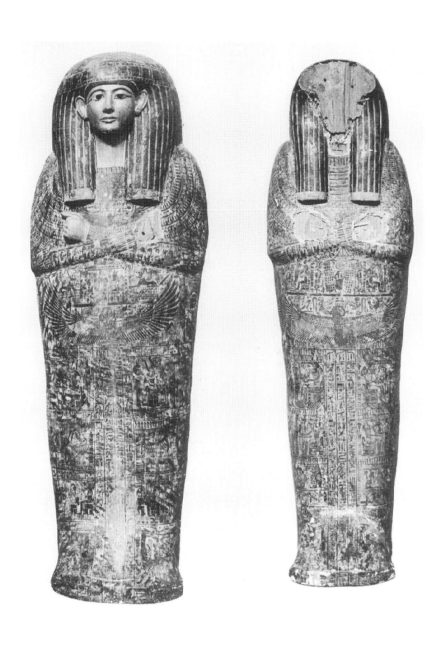

The lids of the first and second coffins of Masaharta (Fig 178)

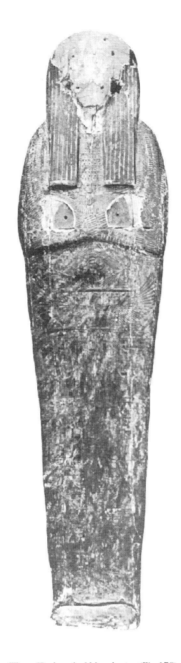

The coffin board of Masaharta (Fig 179)

TAYUHERET. 21st Dynasty. c. 1045 B.C.

Tayuheret was possibly the wife of Masaharta, General and High Priest of Amun.

The Mummy: Found in the Royal Cache at Deir el Bahri in 1881. Cairo Museum Catalogue Number **61041**.

The mummy of Tayuheret was greatly disturbed by robbers who removed every item of value. The body does, however, remain substantially intact. The mummification techniques used are identical to those employed on the other mummies of this period.

The face has been tightly packed with linen, which protrudes from the mouth.

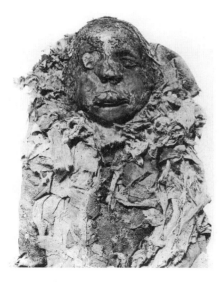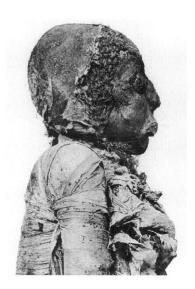

The mummy of Tayuheret (detail) (Figs 180 and 181)

Damage to the skin of the forehead by insects, probably in antiquity, can be seen.

This mummy has not been completely unwrapped and the moulded linen breasts are still in place.

Height of the body 1.606 metres.

The Coffins: Cairo Museum Catalogue Number **61032.**

The set of two sycamore coffins used for Tayuheret were originally made for a Songstress of Amun called Hatel.

Both the coffins (**61032A** and **61032B**) and the coffin board (**61032C**) are a 'set', identical in design and detail. They have been damaged by robbers who have stripped off the gilt hands and faces. The head and feet of the coffin board are completely missing.

Finely painted funerary scenes cover both the exterior and interior of the coffins and the coffin board.

The first coffin: Length 2.18 metres. Breadth 0.71 metres. Height 0.65 metres.

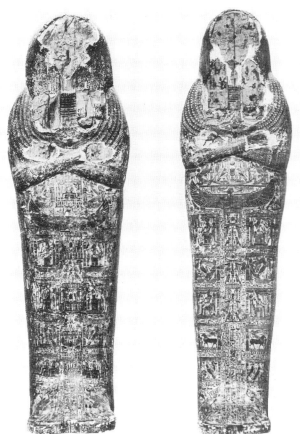

The lids of the first and second coffins of Tayuheret (Fig 182)

The second coffin: Length 2.0 metres. Breadth 0.57 metres. Height 0.67 metres.

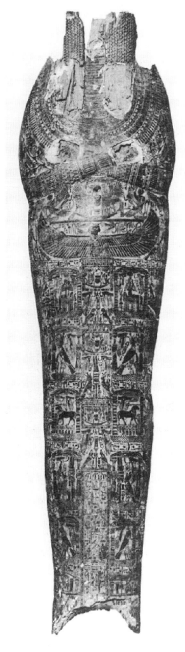

The coffin board of Tayuheret (Fig 183)

The coffin board: Length 1.65 metres. Breadth 0.45 metres.

PINUDJEM II.　　21st Dynasty.　　c. 990-969 B.C.

Pinudjem II was the High Priest of Amun at Thebes.

The Mummy:　Found in the Royal Cache at Deir el Bahri in 1881.
　　　　　　　Cairo Museum Catalogue Number 61094.

The mummy of Pinudjem II is intact, having survived the attentions of tomb robbers. A series of funerary amulets remain on the body.

　　The embalming methods are typical of the period, with the packing giving the body a plump appearance.

Height of the body 1.706 metres.

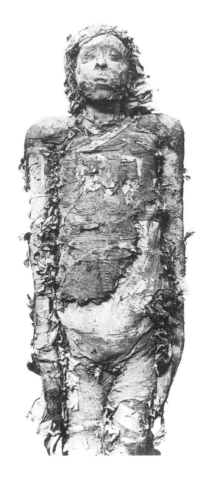

The mummy of Pinudjem II (Detail) (Fig 184)

The Coffins: Cairo Museum Catalogue Number **61029.**

Pinudjem II was found in a set of two coffins, with a coffin board covering the wrapped mummy.

The coffins and Board are those originally made for him and they are all intact.

Gilded hands hold the emblems of the God Osiris and the Goddess Isis.

The gilded faces are framed by large wigs with blue and gold stripes.

The entire surface of each coffin and the board is covered in funerary scenes.

The first coffin: **(61029A)** Length 2.14 metres. Breadth 0.74 metres. Height 0.54 metres.

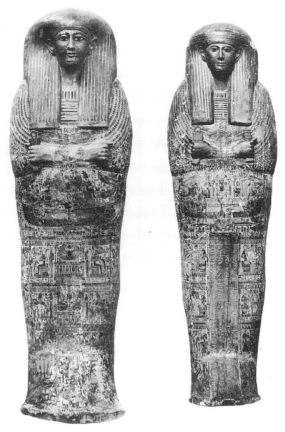

The lids of the first and second coffins of Pinudjem II (Fig 185)

The second coffin: (**61029B**) Length l.95 metres.
Breadth 0.62 metres. Height 0.69 metres.

No measurements are available for the coffin board (**61029C**).

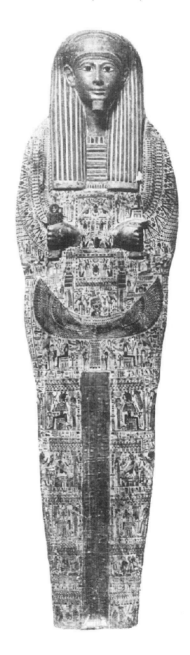

The coffin board of Pinudjem II (Fig 186)

QUEEN ISTEMKHEB.   21st Dynasty   c. 970 B.C.

Istemkheb was a daughter of the High Priest Menkhepere and a wife of Pinudjem II.

From the intact state of her mummy and coffins and the amount of funerary equipment found, it is more than likely that she was buried in Tomb DB 320 on her death.

The Mummy: Found in the Royal Cache at Deir el Bahri in 1881.
Cairo Museum Catalogue Number **61093**.
Exhibition Number **6366**.

The mummy of Queen Istemkheb was so beautifully wrapped by the embalmers that Elliot Smith decided not to unwrap it. The first glimpse beneath the bandages was by the use of X-Rays which revealed a small amulet on the neck and arm, with an unidentified object on her forehead.

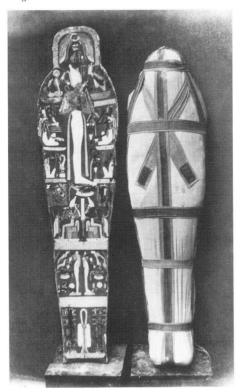

The reverse of the coffin board and the wrapped mummy of Queen Istemkheb (Fig 187)

The teeth are well worn and the molars show what may well have been caries. The third molar appears to have been displaced by some injury.

Istemkheb suffered in life from arthritis in her knees.

Height of the body 1.568 metres.

The Coffins: Cairo Museum Catalogue Number **61031.**

The mummy of Queen Istemkheb was enclosed in two cedar coffins. A wood coffin board covered the wrapped mummy.

The first coffin is intact and is heavily gilded on the face hands and parts of the wig.

The second coffin and coffin board have lost their gilded faces and hands. All are decorated with the usual funerary scenes.

The first coffin; **(61031A).** Length 2.05 metres.
Breadth. 0.68 metres. Height 0.98 metres.

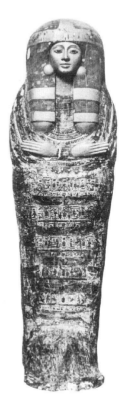

The lid of the first coffin of Queen Istemkheb (Fig 188)

The second coffin: **(61031B)**. Length 1.90 metres.
Breadth 0.55 metres. Height 0.98 metres.

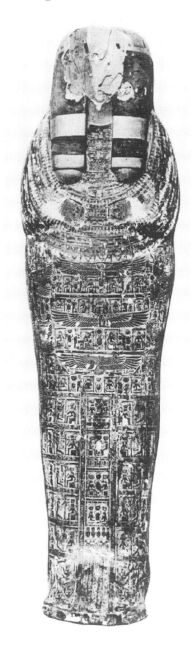

The lid of the second coffin of Queen Istemkheb (Fig 189)

The coffin board: (61031C). Length 1.77 metres.
Breadth 0.445 metres.

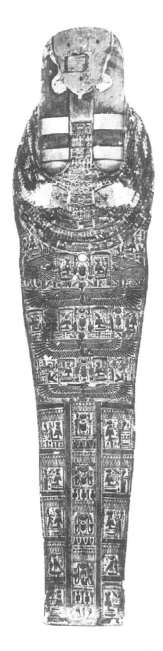

The coffin board of Queen Istemkheb (Fig 190)

QUEEN NESKHONS. 21st Dynasty. c. 970 B.C.

Neskhons was a wife of Pinudjem II.

The Mummy: Found in the Royal Cache at Deir el Bahri in 1881.
Cairo Museum Catalogue Number **61095.**

The mummy of Queen Neskhons is one of the finest examples of the art of embalming in the 21st Dynasty.

The packing of the face and limbs has been skilfully accomplished with none of the over-packing seen in other mummies of this period.

Curiously enough, the embalmers made no attempt to pack the breasts which are flattened and pressed against the body wall.

Height of the body 1.615 metres.

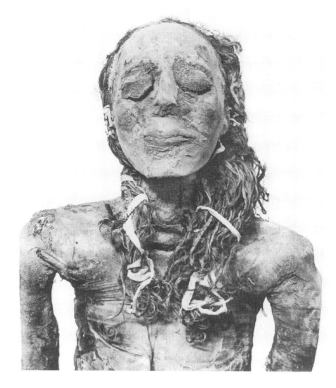

The mummy of Queen Neskhons (detail) (Fig 191)

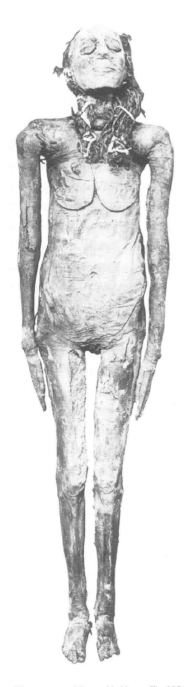

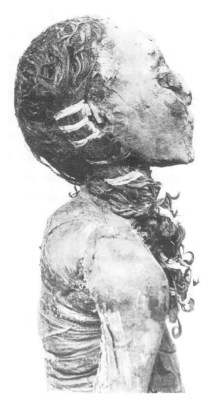

The mummy of Queen Neskhons (detail)
(Fig 193)

The mummy of Queen Neskhons (Fig 192)

The Coffins: Cairo Museum Catalogue Number 61030.

Queen Neskhons was buried in a set of coffins usurped from an individual called Isiemkheb. The two cedar coffins and coffin board are a set and are all of the same design.

The first coffin is intact with the gilded hands and face untouched by robbers. The second coffin and coffin board have lost their hands and faces. It is a curious fact that whereas many of the outer coffins found in the Cache are intact, their inner coffins are invariably damaged. This is possibly because the robbers removed the lids of the outer coffins first, putting them on one side and paying them little attention, in the hope of finding greater riches nearer the bodies. Presumably the outer coffins were then forgotten. It is also possible that the robbers wanted to conceal the fact that the robbery had taken place, at least temporarily. By replacing the outer coffin lids their handiwork would be hidden.

The first coffin (61030A). Length 2.06 metres.
Breadth 0.71 metres. Height 0.74 metres.

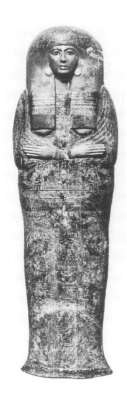

The lid of the first coffin of Queen Neskhons (Fig 194)

The second coffin: (61030B). Length 1.86 metres. Breadth 0.56 metres. Height 0.65 metres.

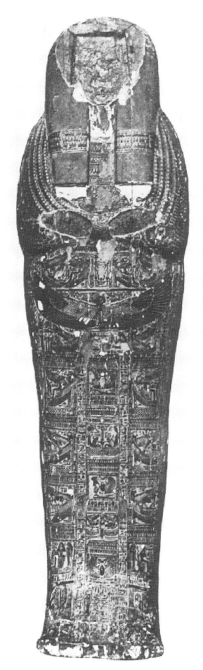

The lid of the second coffin of Queen Neskhons
(Fig 195)

The coffin board (**61030C**). Length 1.78 metres.
Breadth 0.46 metres.

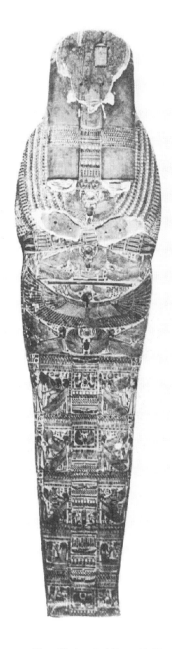 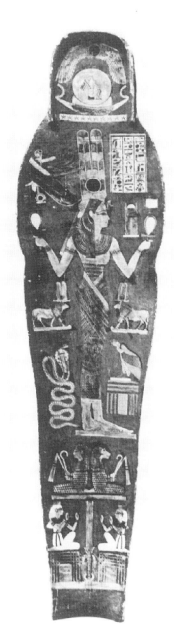

The coffin board of Queen Neskhons: views of the front and back of the board (Fig 196)

NESTANEBTISHRU.   21st Dynasty.   c. 935 B.C.

A Priestess of Amun, Nestanebtishru was a daughter of Pinudjem II and wife of Djedptahiufankh.

The Mummy: Found in the Royal Cache at Deir el Bahri in 1881.
Cairo Museum Catalogue Number **61096.**

The mummy of Nestanebtishru, like that of Neskhons, is also one of the finest of the 21st Dynasty mummies to survive. Once again the packing has been skilfully done in an attempt to restore a lifelike appearance.

Artificial eyes of white stone with black pupils are revealed through the half closed eyelids.

Height of the body 1.620 metres.

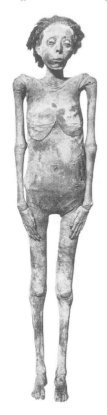

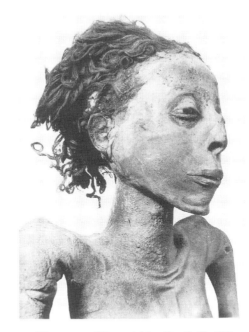

The mummy of Nestanebtishru (detail) (Fig 198)

The mummy of Nestanebtishru (Fig 197)

219

The Coffins: Cairo Museum Catalogue number **61033.**

Compared with the other mummies of this period, the two coffins which contained the mummy of Nestanebtishru are poorly preserved. The first coffin is now covered in a coating of black bituminous paint which has obscured virtually all the painted scenes on the coffin. The second coffin has been treated in the same way, although some of the detail is still visible. These coffins are probably the originals made for Nestanebtishru.

The first coffin: **(61033A).** (Not illustrated).
Length 2.10 metres. Breadth 0.75 metres. Height 0.95 metres.

The second coffin: **(61033B).** Length 1.94 metres.
Breadth 0.57 metres. Height 0.63 metres.

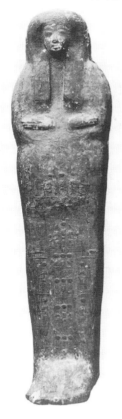

The lid of the second coffin of Nestanebtishru (Fig 199)

The coffin board: **(61033C).** (Not illustrated).
Length 1.56 metres. Breadth 0.42 metres.

DJEDPTAHIUFANKH.　　21st Dynasty.　　c. 935 B.C.

Djedptahiufankh was the husband of Nestanebtishru.

The Mummy:　Found in the Royal Cache at Deir el Bahri in 1881.
　　　　　　　Cairo Museum Catalogue Mumber **61097.**

The mummy of Djedptahiufankh was treated in the same way as that of his wife. Despite the attentions of tomb robbers, several amulets and items of jewellery still remain on the mummy.

The embalming incision is covered by a copper alloy plate.

Artificial eyes have been inserted into the sockets. The face and limbs have been packed to restore the contours of the body.

Height of the body 1.695 metres.

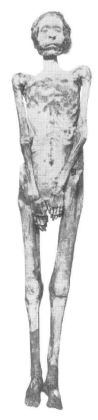

The mummy of Djedptahiufankh (Fig 200)

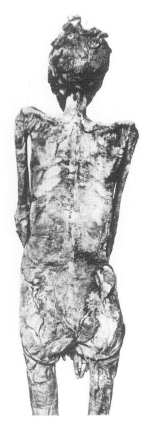

The mummy of Djedptahiufankh (detail) (Fig 201)

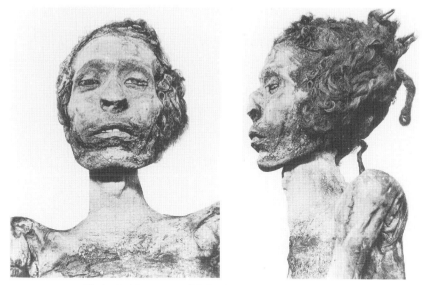

The head of the mummy of Djedptahiufankh (Figs 202 and 203)

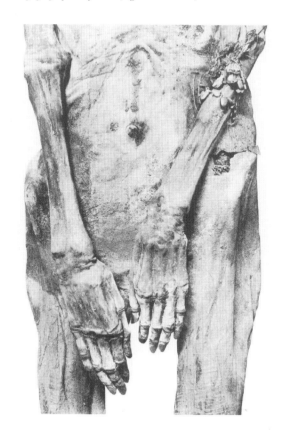

*The mummy of Djedptahiufankh
(Detail) (Fig 204)*

The Coffins: Cairo Museum Catalogue Number **61034.**

The mummy of Djedptahiufankh was found in a set of two coffins made of cedar. A cedar coffin board covered the wrapped mummy. All had been usurped from an individual called Nesshuenopet.

    Apart from a missing hand on the first coffin, all are intact, with the surfaces covered in funerary scenes.

The first coffin: (**61034A**). Length 1.99 metres. Breadth 0.65 metres. Height 0.91 metres.

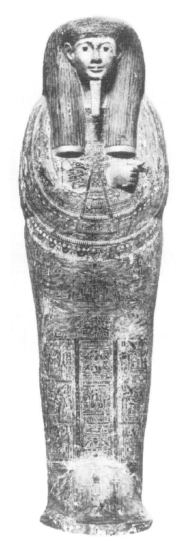

The lid of the first coffin of Djedptahiufankh (Fig 205)

The second coffin: (61034B). Length 1.84 metres.
Breadth 0.53 metres. Height 0.61 metres.

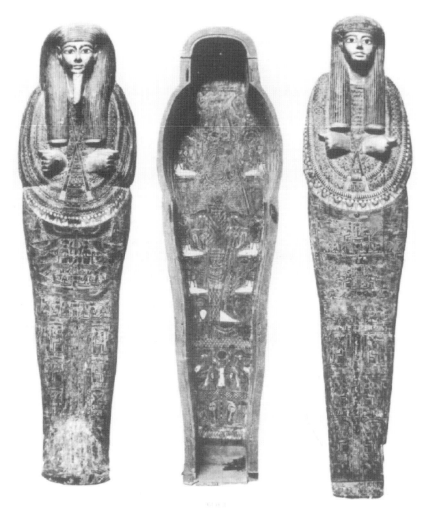

The second coffin and coffin board of Djedptahiufankh (Fig 206)

The coffin board: (61034C). Length 1.74 metres.
Breadth 0.42 metres.

A QUESTION OF MISTAKEN IDENTITY?

The bulk of the collection of Royal mummies in the Cairo Museum (many of which are not on display) were examined by Maspero at the end of the last century and by Elliot Smith at the beginning of this century.

Elliot Smith's catalogue of the mummies covers forty-eight from the two Royal Caches and two found in the tomb of Thutmose III (numbers 61051 and 61000). (These two mummies were considered to be obtrusive later burials and are not included here).

Elliot Smith made many scholarly judgements on the similarity between supposed family-groupings of mummies. In his descriptions and comments he expressed the wish that the newly-discovered X-Rays would be used to examine the mummies and that they might resolve some of the identification problems.

The mummy of Thutmose IV was the first to be examined by X-Rays in 1903.

The wrapped mummy of Amenhotep I was X-Rayed by Dr. Douglas Derry in February 1932. In 1965 a major X-Ray examination of some of the Royal mummies was made by an American team, led by Kent Weeks and James Harris. Using portable X-Ray equipment, the X-Rays were made without removing the mummies from their glass-covered display cases.

The X-Rays revealed much information about the Royal mummies, but also posed many problems.

Some individual mummies show obviously different characteristics from their immediate predecessors and their successors, which indicates that these mummies may have been incorrectly identified by the ancient priests who arranged the re-burials.

Mummies which do not appear to 'fit' include Ahmose and Thutmose I. Amenhotep II and Amenhotep III also present features inconsistent wth their supposed fathers and sons. Elliot Smith considered that the mummy of Seti II resembled the mummies of the Thutmoside Kings and that the embalming technique used was of the 18th Dynasty rather than the 19th.

Using the X-Rays of the mummies, Edward Wente and James Harris led a team of investigators who looked at the craniofacial variations of the mummies.

The 17th and 18th Dynasty mummies appear to be largely a heterogeneous group, with long craniums and delicate features when compared with the 19th and 20th Dynasty groups.

Using the position of the arms of some of the mummies as a guide and comparison of the craniofacial features, a tentative re-identification of some of the mummies has been possible.

The craniofacial features are important in this identification technique. We all inherit features from our parents and pass on features to our children. It is usual for there to be some similarity between the features of parents and children. The comparisons of the features of some of the Royal mummies has highlighted some individuals who are possibly wrongly identified because their facial features could not have been inherited from their known parents and have not been passed on to their known children.

The mummies identified as Thutmose II and Seti II are possibly really those of Thutmose I and II. It is also unlikely that Amenhotep II could be the son of the mummy called Thutmose III. This could mean that Amenhotep II is really Thutmose IV and Thutmose IV, Amenhotep III.

The mummy we know as Amenhotep III whose features exhibit an extraordinary deviation in craniofacial features, would then have to be assigned to an unrelated king, such as Ay or Horemheb (whose mummies are both 'missing').

There is a problem here, however, for the mummy of Thutmose IV is one of the best-identified of the Royal mummies. If this identification is indeed correct, an alternative sequence is possible:-

Thutmose III is either Thutmose III or Amenhotep II. Thutmose IV remains Thutmose IV. Amenhotep II becomes Amenhotep III and Amenhotep III becomes Akhenaten (this mummy exhibits quite brutal destruction, which is inconsistent with the depredations of tomb robbers). Since the body from Tomb KV 55 and Tutankhamun are unlikely biological sons of either Amenhotep III or Akhenaten, as represented by the mummies of Amenhotep II and III, it is tentatively suggested that Amenhotep III and Thutmose IV were the maternal and paternal grandfathers respectively of Smenkhkare and Tutankhamun.

...Confusing isn't it? Clearly some of the mummies have been wrongly identified for the last three thousand years.

Only further scientific research will once and for all resolve this problem, confirm the identity of the supposedly known mummies and possibly also correctly identify those whose identity is in dispute. It is even possible that some 'missing' Royal mummies may be identified.

Whatever the outcome of such research, the description of the mummies and their coffins included in this volume will still be valid with the names waiting to be added or amended as and when further information is available.

From the evidence of the mummies and the details written on the coffins and wrappings by the priests of the 21st Dynasty, it is possible to appreciate the difficulty of their task in arranging the re-burials.

The Royal tombs were always a prime target for robbers and no tomb has completely escaped. Even the tomb of Tutankhamun was broken into at least twice. The Necropolis officials hastily packed items back into boxes and re-sealed the tomb.

In tombs where the mummy had been robbed, the officials re-wrapped the body and presumably would have left it in the original tomb which would have been re-sealed. At some stage, presumably because of further robberies, the mummies were collected together in various tombs for greater protection. It was when these communal tombs were robbed, yet again, that the restoration of the burials caused particular difficulties: several mummies may have been removed from their coffins and wrappings. The priests had to attempt to identify the bodies and replace them in their respective coffins. In some cases the mummies were lost completely, in others the coffins were also missing, or too damaged to use. Other coffins were collected for use, some of which had been used for earlier burials, both Royal and non-Royal.

The whole operation would, no doubt, have been carried out in secret and with some urgency. Small wonder, therefore, that the identification of some of the bodies is uncertain, or that other bodies have remained unidentified.

Some of the work of the re-burial parties may well have been undertaken at Medinet Habu, site of the palace and temple of Ramesses III.

It is of course possible that the mummies were laid to rest with the full knowledge of the local community, it having been made clear and obvious that nothing of any value was being re-buried with the bodies. Indeed, it is thought that the stripping of the gold from some of the Royal coffins, was done by the priests themselves, perhaps to ensure that nothing of value remained to lure the robbers, or perhaps for other reasons.

John Romer discovered evidence in the tomb of Ramesses XI in the Valley of the Kings, which indicates that some of this work may have taken place there. Fragments of items from several Royal burials were found in this tomb, all stripped of their gold. The Priest-Kings of the 21st Dynasty obviously considered that the location of the main tomb chosen to house a collection of Royal mummies, was secure and chose to be buried there themselves. Many of their burials are virtually intact, but there was relatively little of any actual value buried with them in the form of jewellery or other precious items. The gold on their coffins was only stripped in the last century when the location of the tomb was re-discovered. It was the smaller objects from these burials, such as ushabti, which alerted Egyptologists to the discovery of the first Cache.

WHAT DID THEY REALLY LOOK LIKE?

Although we can look into the faces of the mummies of some of the greatest Pharaohs of Egypt, their appearance in life would have been different.

The mummification process removes all the moisture from the body causing it to lose most of its bulk. This is most apparent in the limbs of the mummies which (apart from the later mummies where subcutaneous packing was introduced) are little more than skin and bone.

The features of the face always appear to be the best preserved, for the layer of skin and tissue over the bones is relatively thin. The skin becomes stretched over the bones and whilst the face will retain many of its features it is not always possible to say, for example, if the individual was plump or wrinkled. The bandaging of the head also distorts many features; noses in particular are often flattened by the pressure of tightly wrapped bandages or by packing of the nostrils.

A few attempts have been made to show the lifelike appearance of some of the Royal mummies. The most notable results were achieved by artist Winifred Brunton, who in the Nineteen Twenties completed a superb series of small paintings of Kings and Queens and other important figures from Ancient Egypt. She used the evidence of the mummies where possible, but also referred to examples of sculpture for some of the figures.

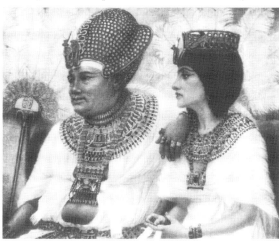

Amenhotep III and Queen Tiye: Portrait painted by Winifred Brunton (Fig 207)

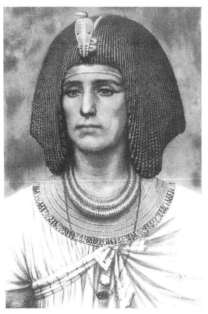

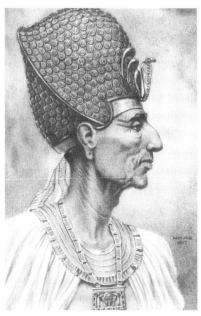

Seti I: Portrait painted by Winifred Brunton (Fig 208)

Ramesses II: Portrait painted by Winifred Brunton (Fig 209)

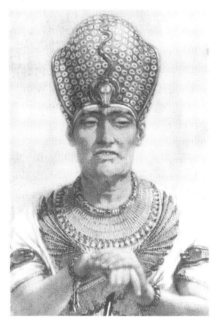

Ramesses III: Portrait painted by Winifred Brunton (Fig 210)

Modern techniques now enable even more accurate reconstructions to be made. Manchester Museum, as part of the extensive scientific investigation of their collection of mummies, used a technique based on the use of casts of the skulls of three of them. Richard Neave, who is Assistant Director of the Department of Medical Illustration at the University of Manchester, built up new 'flesh' of clay on the skull casts. The thickness of the flesh was based on anatomical research on human heads. This technique was originally used by the police, to good effect, to identify murder victims where only skeletons remained.

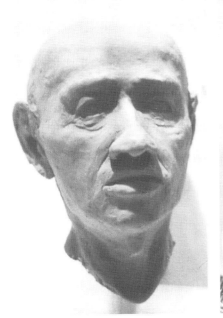 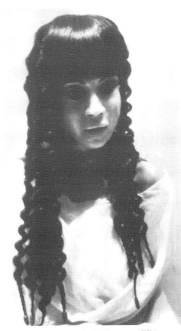

Reconstructed head of Nekht-Ankh:
Manchester Museum (Fig 211)

Reconstructed head of Mummy 1770:
Manchester Museum (Fig 212)

The results were striking. Although some details, such as the shape of the ears and nose, cannot be reconstructed accurately when only a skull is available, the features of the reconstructed heads almost brought the Ancient Egyptians to life. For the first time we could see what they probably really looked like.

Other museums in this country and around the world soon followed suit, using some of their more badly damaged mummies where the skulls were available. The next logical step was to use X-Ray tomography to build up an image of the skull which can then be reproduced in three dimensions and then used as the basis for a reconstruction in clay. This technique means that the mummies are not damaged and even the features of wrapped mummies can be reconstructed in this way.

The Yorvick Viking Centre at York has taken the use of

technology still further by generating a reconstructed face on a computer which has been fed with details of the skull measurements. Such reconstructions can be made to reproduce on screen the image of a three dimensional object. The information can then be used to produce an actual three dimensional reproduction.

Clearly there is great potential to make accurate reconstructions of the features of the Pharaohs. Skull measurements and X-Rays have already been taken, but techniques have improved dramatically over the last ten years or so and new X-Rays and scans of the mummies would need to be made. With well preserved mummies, details such as the shape of the ears and nose are available, plus other evidence of the age and physical condition of the individual. All this wealth of data would enable detailed and more accurate representations to be made. The appeal is great and hopefully it will only be a matter of time before someone undertakes this work in conjunction with a more scientific investigation.

OTHER ROYAL TOMBS OF THE 21ST AND 22ND DYNASTIES

In addition to the various discoveries of Royal Tombs at Luxor, the site of Ancient Thebes, a group of Royal tombs was discovered in the Delta city of Tanis in 1939, by the French Egyptologist Pierre Montet. The discovery received little publicity at the time because of the outbreak of the Second World War. Excavations were hurried and were abandoned, not being resumed until 1945.

Six Royal Tombs were found in the south-west corner of the huge temple complex of Amun. The burials dated from the 21st and 22nd Dynasties and are contemporary with some of the Royal burials made at Thebes.

Three of the tombs had been completely plundered in antiquity, but the remaining three burials were intact and large amounts of gold and silver objects, including coffins and funeral masks were found.

Sadly, the contents of the tombs had suffered badly from the seepage of water into the underground chambers. Whilst all the stone and metal objects were well preserved, little organic matter survived. The mummies were little more than skeletons, covered in items of jewellery and decayed wrappings.

The Tanis mummies are not included in this volume. Few good photographs are available and the remains have not received the attention that the better preserved Theban mummies have in recent years. Hopefully this will be rectified in the future. The family relationships between the Tanis and Theban rulers is complex and much could be resolved by a full scientific examination.

The actual remains had for many years been 'lost', but they have recently been rediscovered in the University of Cairo.

Included in the Bibliograpby are various volumes which give accounts of the discovery of the tombs at Tanis and descriptions of the objects found.

ARE THERE ROYAL TOMBS AND MUMMIES STILL TO BE FOUND?

Yes. There are a number of Kings and Queens for whom no tombs and no mummies are known. There are also a number of Royal mummies found in the Royal Caches where the location of the original tomb is still unknown.

The Royal Necropolis at Thebes is vast and although it has been searched and excavated almost continually for over one hundred years, there must remain the possibility of the discovery of new tombs, although the likelihood of finding un-plundered tombs is always slim.

The emphasis of archaeological work today has changed from the early years of this century. Conservation now is one of the main aims and the Valley of the Kings has particular problems, caused not only by the vast number of tourists visiting the tombs, but by continuing excavation in geologically unstable parts of the Valley.

The days of archaeologists looking specifically for objects, particularly for works of art to display in Museums and for the collections of wealthy patrons, have long gone. Most Egyptologists, however, probably have dreams of making a spectacular discovery. Such dreams are important and one day, someone will be lucky.

It is possible that there are other Royal mummies to be found, and their identification might not necessarily entail the discovery of new tombs. It is apparent that there was some confusion about the identity of some of the mummies when the first Royal Cache was discovered. Original accounts recorded the mummy of Pinudjem I, but there was no such mummy recorded by the time the Official Catalogue was produced. In the rapid clearance of the tomb and the transportation of the mummies to Cairo, were some 'lost' in the storage rooms of the Cairo Museum or possibly the University of Cairo?

Were any mummies removed from the Royal Cache *before* the official discovery? This was a time when mummies were prized as souvenirs of visits to Egypt and it is not impossible that mummies were removed from the Cache before the full importance of the discovery was realised. The truth will probably never be known, but if crossed arms are an attribute specific to Royal mummies, there are two possible candidates for the 'lost' Pharaohs. There is a male mummy, now in the Niagara Falls Museum, and another in the Rosicrucian Museum at San José. Both date from the correct period and were obtained in Egypt at the end of the last century. Could these be Horemheb, Ay, Ramesses VIII or Setnakht? Are there other mummies lying in museums around the world which came from the Deir el Bahri Cache?

Many other mummies still lie in some of the smaller and undecorated tombs in the Valley of the Kings. Tomb KV21 was first discovered by Giovanni Belzoni in 1817 and was found to contain two uncoffined female mummies. This and other tombs discovered during the last century and the beginning of this century contained only fragments of burial equipment and damaged mummies, which proved to be of little interest to the early explorers and Egyptologists. They removed what objects were of interest and abandoned the tombs. In many instances, debris soon covered the entrances and the precise location of these tombs was lost.

Donald Ryan has been re-locating and re-opening many of these smaller tombs and he has found a large number of mummies, including females and children, mostly damaged, whose identification is not known. It is possible that some may be the original occupants of Royal tombs - not necessarily the tombs in which they were found, for we know that many of the mummies were moved to other tombs after the original burials had been robbed.

The two female mummies, for example, in tomb KV21 can now be studied again. Both may be Royal for their arms are in the supposed 'Royal' position as shown in the mummy of Queen Tiye and possibly the female mummy in KV60.

There is much work still to be done in this area; the use of X-Rays and a full scientific examination of mummies may provide the answers and finally give us clues as to the identity of these people.

SELECT BIBLIOGRAPHY

ADAMS, Barbara. *Egyptian Mummies.* Shire Publications, 1984.

ANDREWS, Carol. *Egyptian Mummies.* British Museum Publications, 1984.

ALDRED, Cyril. *Akhenaten King of Egypt.* Thames and Hudson, 1988.

BALOUT. Lionel and ROUBET, Prof. C. *La Momie de Ramses II.* Edition Récherche Sur les Civilisations, 1985.

BRUNTON, Winifred. *Kings and Queens of Ancient Egypt.* Hodder and Stoughton, 1921.

BRUNTON, Winifred. *Great Ones of Ancient Egypt.* Hodder and Stoughton, 1929.

BRYAN, Betsy M. *The Reign of Thutmose IV.* John Hopkins University Press, 1991.

BRYAN, Betsy M., KOZLOF; Arielle P. and others. *Egypts Dazzling Sun: Amenhotep III and his World.* Cleveland Museum of Art, 1992.

CARTER, Howard and MACE, Arthur C. *The Tomb of Tutankhamen.* Cassell and Co. 1923.

DARESSY, Georges. *Cercueils des Cachettes Royales* Cairo Museum, 1912.

DARESSY, Georges. *Fouilles de la Vallée des Rois.* Cairo Museum, 1902.

DAVID, A. Rosalie. *Mysteries of the Mummies.* Book Club Associates, 1978.

DAVID, A. Rosalie. *The Manchester Museum Mummy Project.* Manchester University Press, 1979.

DAVID, A. Rosalie and Antony E. *A Biographical Dictionary of Ancient Egypt.* B.A. Seaby, 1992.

DAVID, A. Rosalie and TAPP, Eddie. *Evidence Embalmed.* Manchester University Press, 1984.

DAVIS, Theodore and MASPERO, Gaston. *The Tomb of Iouiya and Touiyou.* Archibald Constable and Co, 1907.

DAVIS, Theodore and others. *The Tomb of Queen Ti.* KMT Communications 1991.

DAWSON, Warren
and UPHILL, Eric.

Who was Who in Egyptlogy.
The Egypt Exploration Society,1972.

EDWARDS, I.E.S.

Tutankhamun, His Tomb and its Treasures.
Victor Gollancz, 1979.

ELLIOT SMITH, Grafton.

The Royal Mummies. Cairo Museum,
1909.

ELLIOT-SMITH, Grafton
and DAWSON, Warren.

Egyptian Mummies. Kegan Paul. 1991.

EL MAHDY, Christine.

*Mummies, Myth and Magic in Ancient
Egypt.* Thames and Hudson, 1989.

FREED, Rita.

Ramses the Great. Boston Museum of
Science, 1988.

HARRIS, James E.
and WENTE, Edward F.

An X-Ray Atlas of the Royal Mummies.
University of ChicagoPress, 1980.

HARRIS, James
and WEEKS, Kent R.

X-Raying the Pharaohs'. Macdonald,
1973.

HOBSON, Christine.

Exploring the World of the Pharaohs.
Guild Publishing, 1987.

KAMIL, Jill.

Upper Egypt. Longman Group, 1983.

LEEK, F. Filce.

*The Human Remains from the Tomb of
Tutankamun.* Griffith Institute, 1972.

LINDEN-SMITH, Joseph

Tombs, Temples and Egyptian Art.
University of Oklahoma Press 1956'.

MANNICHE, Lise.

An Ancient Egyptian Herbal. British
Museum Publications, 1989.

MASPERO, Gaston.

The Struggle of Nations. SPCK, 1896.

MASPERO, Gaston.

New Light on Ancient Egypt. T. Fisher
Unwin, 1909.

MASPERO, Gaston
and BRUGSCH, Emile.

La Trouvaille de Deir d Bahari. Cairo
Museum, 1881.

MOBERLY-BELL, C.F.

From Pharaohs to Fellahs. Wells, Gardner,
Darton and Co, 1888.

MURMANE, William J.

The Penguin Guide to Ancient Egypt.
Penguin Books, 1983.

OSMAN, Ahmed.

Stranger in the Valley of the Kings.
Souvenir Press, 1987.

PATERSON, James
Hamilton and
ANDREWS, Carol.

Mummies. British Museum Publications,
1978.

QUIBELL, J.

The Tomb of Yuaa and Thuiu. Cairo
Museum, 1908.

REEVES, Carole.   *Egyptian Medicine.* Shire Publications,
                                   1992.
REEVES, C. Nicholas.   *The Valley of the Kings.* Kegan Paul, 1990.
REEVES, C. Nicholas.   *The Complete Tutankhamun.* Thames and
                                   Hudson, 1990.
REEVES C. Nicholas.   *After Tutankhamun.* Kegan Paul, 1992.
ROBINS, G. and   *The Physical Proportions and Living*
    SHUTE, C.C.D.   *Stature of New Kingdom Pharaohs.* The
                                   Journal of Human Evolution, Volume
                                   12, Number 5, July 1983.
ROSE, John.   *The Sons of Re.* J.R.T. Warrington.
ROMER, John.   *Valley of the Kings.* Book Club
                                   Associates, 1981.
SALEH, Mohamed and   *The Egyptian Museum, Cairo.* Cairo
    SOUROUZIAN, Hourig.   Museum, 1987.
THOMAS, Elizabeth.   *The Royal Necropoleis of Thebes.*
                                   Princeton, 1966.
WINLOCK, H.E.   *The Tomb of Queen Meryet-Amun at*
                                   Thebes. Metropolitan Museum of Art,
                                   1930.

Sundry Publications

A Guide to the Egyptian Museum, Cairo.
Cairo Museum, 1976.

Gold of The Pharaohs. City of Edinburgh
Museum and Art Gallery, 1988.

K.M.T. Magazine, volumes 1 to 13. KMT
Communications San Francisco 1990/
1991/ 1992/1993.

After Tutankamun. Abstract of papers
and presentations of the International
Conference, 1990.

INDEX

Note: Numbers in **bold** indicate the main reference to the mummy or coffin of specific individuals.

LIST OF SPONSORS

Publication of this book was made much easier because of the generous sponsorship of the following people, who in addition to their encouragement, also contributed in real terms to cover the cost of re-photographing the original photographs of the Royal mummies and coffins. I would also like to thank the attendees of the Northern meetings of the Egypt Exploration Society in Manchester, whose contributions to my *Egyptology* Newsletter have helped cover some of the costs incurred in preparing this book.

Martin Abbott
Victor Blunden
Allan F. Boley
Christine Brown
Audrey Carter
Paul Clarke
Alison and Ian Cole
Rebecca Cole
Peter Coppack
Tim East
Pauline English
Mark Gardiner
Bill and Karen Griffiths
Chris Guy
Tony and Joyce Harkus
John and Kathleen Holden
Paul Hill
Ian and Marion Johnstone

Jill McKeown
Martin McCrory (Books B.C.)
Richard and Lesley Milner
Phil and Jill Morrish
Simon Morrish
Ian Musgrove
Bernard and Mary Partridge
Brian Pearson
Phil Pettit
Peter Phillips
Gerard Pfirsch
Gordon Ross
Manfred Schulte
Kent Sproule
Wisdom Stanley
Jon Tarrant
Pamela Taylor
Margaret Trewin
Herbie Weiner
ley